The Commissioner

The
Commissioner

A True Story of Deceit, Dishonor, and Death

BILL KEITH

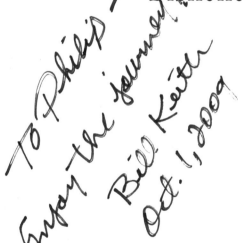

To Philip's —
Enjoy the journey
Bill Keith
Oct. 1, 2009

PELICAN PUBLISHING COMPANY
GRETNA 2009

*The word "Pelican" and the depiction of a pelican are trademarks
of Pelican Publishing Company, Inc., and are registered in the
U.S. Patent and Trademark Office.*

Library of Congress Cataloging-in-Publication Data

Keith, Bill, 1934-
  The commissioner : a true story of deceit, dishonor, and death /
Bill Keith.
    p. cm.
  Includes bibliographical references.
    ISBN 978-1-58980-655-9 (hardcover : alk. paper) 1. Murder—
Louisiana—Shreveport—Case studies. 2. Murder—Investigation—
Shreveport—Case studies. I. Title.
  HV6533.L8K45 2009
  364.152'3092—dc22
                                2008052115

Printed in the United States of America

Published by Pelican Publishing Company, Inc.
1000 Burmaster Street, Gretna, Louisiana 70053

To the so-called "Dirty Five," a.k.a. Shreveport's "Untouchables"—Police Chief T. P. Kelley, Chief of Detectives Kenneth Lanigan, Detective Major James Byrd, Detective Captain Sam Burns, and Detective Lieutenant Robert Merolla—all former policemen who many years ago saved the City of Shreveport from the tyrannical rule of a dangerous lawman and the specter of organized crime.

Contents

Prologue 11

Chapter One: A Killing in Louisiana 15

Chapter Two: The Story 29

Chapter Three: Prelude to Evil 35

Chapter Four: A Secret Meeting 53

Chapter Five: Law and Disorder 61

Chapter Six: D'Artois, the Lawman 79

Chapter Seven: The Missing Records 91

Chapter Eight: A New Twist, a Big Surprise 103

Chapter Nine: The Grand Jury 113

Chapter Ten: The Hit Man 127

Chapter Eleven: The Last Hurrah! 135

Chapter Twelve: Tales of Treachery and Intrigue 143

Chapter Thirteen: The Murder of Rusty Griffith 151

Chapter Fourteen: Standoff at the D'Artois Home 159

Chapter Fifteen: The Affidavit 175

Chapter Sixteen: Justice vs. Politics 181

Chapter Seventeen: The Last Roll Call 189

Chapter Eighteen: The D'Artois Day in Court 193

Epilogue 197

Appendix A: The Legacy 203

Appendix B: The Legacy Continues—Crooks and
Other Scoundrels 217

Notes 231

The price good men pay for indifference to public affairs is to be ruled by evil men.
—Plato

Prologue

A gentle breeze carried wave after wave of warm air across the state capital from the quiet waters of the Mississippi River as the legendary river, powerful and beautiful, made its way through the city on its long journey to the sea.

The streets of Baton Rouge, Louisiana, were virtually deserted in the early morning hours of July 9, 1976, as Jim Leslie, a young advertising executive from Shreveport, drove toward the historic old Prince Murat Inn only blocks away. He was tired and fighting sleep to stay awake. It had been a long day.

When he turned off Nicholson Drive into the rear parking lot of the Prince Murat, he saw only one vacant parking space near an old six-foot wooden fence, with several strands of barbed wire around the top, almost hidden in the darkness. He parked and locked his car and walked toward the back entrance of the motel.

Two men lurked in the shadows behind the wooden fence. One of them aimed a twelve-gauge shotgun, loaded with OO buckshot, through a crack in the fence and shot Leslie in the back. He reeled to one side and fell face down to the asphalt parking lot and was dead before he hit the ground.

As blood inched slowly around his body and turned a small portion of the parking lot crimson red, the two assassins jumped into a car, wrapped the shotgun in a blanket, and disappeared into the dark night.

The Commissioner

Shreveport advertising executive Jim Leslie was gunned down in the parking lot of the Prince Murat Inn in Baton Rouge. (Courtesy LSUS Archives—Noel Memorial Library)

CHAPTER ONE

A Killing in Louisiana

It was just a nothing kind of day. It was not Pres. Gerald Ford's birthday, Independence Day, or Fat Tuesday. None of my friends was going to Natchez, Mississippi, to Cock of the Walk restaurant to eat catfish or to the coast to hang out on the beach.

A few minutes before seven in the morning, I was drinking my first cup of coffee, trying to wake up and get a grip on the new day. Since I worked late nights as a reporter for the *Shreveport Times* newspaper five and sometimes six nights a week, my early morning ritual generally included a cup of coffee or two and maybe even three.

Each morning I listened to the seven o'clock news program from KEEL Radio in Shreveport to get some idea of what was going on in our city on the banks of the Red River. I could almost predict the news: the scorching temperature in the one hundreds, the farmers' concern over the lack of rain on their cotton and soybean crops on the fertile Red River delta north of the city, a few arrests from the police blotter, and an occasional fire.

We lived in a white frame house near a grove of giant pine trees on a hill overlooking the south shore of Caddo Lake. The lake was located about seventeen miles north of Shreveport near the picturesque little town of Mooringsport. As I waited to hear the news, I poured another cup of coffee and glanced out the kitchen window at the Drift In Landing Marina down by the lake. I saw several fishermen already backing their expensive bass boats into the water. They were going after the elusive trophy bass to stuff, hang in the dens of their homes, and brag about the rest of their lives. And they were getting an early start to try to dodge the heat wave that hit us each summer.

Suddenly that nothing kind of day turned into a day I will never forget. The KEEL reporter had just received a news bulletin out of Baton Rouge alleging that an assassin had killed Shreveport advertising man Jim Leslie.

"Jim Leslie has been murdered!" I yelled to my wife Lowayne who was still in bed. "He was shot in a motel parking lot in Baton Rouge!"

"Surely not," she said, as she joined me in the kitchen.

"Yes, it's true."

We huddled around the radio and listened to the rest of the alarming story. The reporter said that the early indications were that a hit man with ties to organized labor had killed him. Leslie was the architect of the public relations and advertising campaign for the Louisiana Right-to-Work Law—which was strongly opposed by labor forces in the state—that cleared the Louisiana Senate just a few hours before he was killed.

By the time the report ended, I was trembling and could hardly dial the telephone to call the *Times'* newsroom to see if anyone had more information. When I finally collected my thoughts and dialed the number, there was no one at the city desk, but the switchboard operator told me that details were still sketchy.

Although I tried to control my emotions, I wanted to cry out, "What devil from hell would do something like that to a good man like Jim Leslie?"

I was well aware that life is fragile. I learned that one Christmas night when I was covering the police beat for the newspaper and, around midnight, we heard a report over the police scanner that there was a jumper on Twelve Mile Bayou just north of downtown Shreveport.

It was bitter cold with a temperature near zero, and a brisk wind was blowing in from the north when I drove up to Twelve Mile to do a story on the apparent suicide. When I slid out of my car, the snow flurries hit me in the face and the freezing north wind cut through my trench coat and chilled me to the bone. I pulled the coat tighter around my neck, but it didn't help much.

The bayou was an eerie place at night with its murky waters and nearby trees covered with snow and a few saber-toothed icicles. I was amazed by something I saw there that night and didn't know what to think about it. There was a pair of woman's shoes, a purse, and a coat laid out in perfect order there on the bridge over the bayou. Was the jumper trying to leave some message to her family or friends? I wondered. Or perhaps for the police who would investigate her disappearance? Or the divers from the fire department who would search for her body in the icy waters?

My mind was racing at warp speed, but I couldn't comprehend the mental anguish and pain that would cause a woman to jump into the bayou waters to end her life on Christmas night. Neither could I understand the cold-blooded murder of Jim Leslie in the heat of the night in a motel parking lot in Baton Rouge. It was as though evil dropped right down into the middle of the history of our state the night he was killed.

For some time those two events, like a nightmare in slow motion, haunted me like a dirge at midnight and tolled through my soul.

I remembered when I was a war correspondent and first arrived at the Tan Son Nhat Airport in Saigon, Vietnam, in 1967. One of the first things I saw when I left the plane was a sign over the base chapel that read, "Life Is Fragile, Handle with Prayer." When I heard that Leslie was dead and remembered the jumper on Christmas night, I thought once again of that gentle reminder from Vietnam.

Although I was not scheduled to go to work until after lunch, I told my wife, "I'm going on to the newspaper. McDaniel may want me to write the story." Raymond McDaniel was the tough-as-nails, no-nonsense editor of the *Shreveport Times*.

"Just be careful," she said with a hint of sadness in her voice.

I hugged and kissed our children good-bye and departed for Shreveport in my patriotic red, white, and blue Chevrolet Vega with American flags painted on both rear fenders. The Vega needed a ring job and continually puffed smoke, sometimes black and sometimes white, out of the tail pipe. That car was a joke among some of my friends at the newspaper who never understood why the smoke changed colors.

Driving down Louisiana Highway 1 through the pine-covered hills of Northwest Louisiana and past an occasional oil well, there were a number of questions racing through my mind but no answers. Why was Leslie killed? Did it really have anything to do with the right-to-work legislation as reported on KEEL Radio? Later there was some speculation that *Mafia don* Carlos Marcello, who ran the organized crime syndicate in New Orleans, was behind the murder.

When I walked into the newsroom, the atmosphere was like a mortuary during a wake. Everyone was just hanging out in clusters here and there, some around the city desk or in front of McDaniel's office waiting to hear something, anything that would explain the tragic death of Jim Leslie. They had grief and sadness written all over their faces and some of the women were weeping. Others were speaking in hushed tones or saying nothing at all.

Several of the reporters and other staff remembered when Leslie was one of them and worked there in the newsroom as a reporter for the *Times*. They glanced at the desk where he once sat and the typewriter he used to write hundreds of stories. They could almost see the happy-go-lucky Leslie with his gentle smile walking into the newsroom and greeting his friends or rushing out of the newsroom to cover a story for the next morning's edition.

John Hill and Marsha Shuler, our capital correspondents in Baton Rouge, kept us informed during the early hours of the investigation as Baton Rouge detectives began their probe into the execution-style killing. This would become one of the highest profile murder cases in Louisiana history, second only to the assassination of former governor Huey Pierce Long who had been killed in a hallway at the state capitol in 1935, forty-one years earlier.

Hill later told me a friend called him during the predawn hours, arousing him from a deep sleep, to inform him Leslie had been killed. "Of course I was shocked to hear the bad news; it was five o'clock in the morning," Hill said during an interview with me years later. "I had spent a half hour talking to him on a sofa near the senate chambers during the right-to-work debate [on Thursday afternoon]."

Hill and Shuler arrived at the scene of the crime early that morning and saw Leslie's body lying on the asphalt parking lot behind the motel. Both of them had worked with Leslie at the *Shreveport Times* before he resigned from the newspaper to enter the fast-paced world of public relations and advertising. It was difficult for them to deal with seeing their former colleague there on the asphalt lifeless in a pool of blood.

They examined the old wooden fence in the back of the parking lot, with the strands of barbed wire around the top, and saw the opening in the fence through which the detectives believed the fatal shot was fired. It was apparent to both reporters that someone had removed a board to get a clear view of Leslie when he arrived back at the Prince Murat where they killed him.

Through my own personal interviews and various newspaper reports, and in consultation with Hill and Shuler, I have pieced together a sequence of the events that led up to Leslie's murder and the long and difficult investigation that followed.

Although the thirty-eight-year-old advertising executive was dog-tired and fighting to stay awake as he returned to the Prince Murat in the early morning hours, he felt a deep sense of fulfillment as he pondered the events of the day. He had been on pins and needles all day and into the night as he paced back and forth in the senate chambers and listened to the nerve-jangling rhetoric as the senators debated the right-to-work bill with deep passion and old-fashioned southern oratory. However, throughout the intense debate, he had a gut feeling the lawmakers would pass the legislation. But whatever the outcome, he had done his best and had been paid a huge fee for his statewide public relations and advertising campaign on behalf of the bill.

When the president of the senate pounded the gavel and

announced that the bill had been approved on final passage by a majority of the lawmakers, the supporters in the galleries whistled, cheered, and applauded the decision. Leslie breathed a sigh of relief. It had been a long and grueling campaign.

That night the victors held a party at the Camelot Club on the top floor of the Louisiana National Bank building in downtown Baton Rouge for the friendly legislators and the hundreds of businessmen from throughout the state who had come to Baton Rouge to support right to work. It was the kind of party the legislators looked forward to after a hard day's work with plenty of Cajun food and free booze.

There was a spirit of euphoria throughout the club as the men and women stood in line to shake hands with the young advertising executive from Shreveport who had helped them win the important legislative victory.

Sometime after one o'clock in the morning, he said good night to his friends. He hoped to get a few hours sleep at the Prince Murat before returning to Shreveport later in the morning. As he drove through the deserted streets of the capital city, events of the day flashed through his mind like a silent movie. A faint grin creased his face as he thought about the chaotic and unruly atmosphere in the Louisiana Senate chambers earlier in the evening. He could still hear the shouts and catcalls from the packed galleries as the colorful senators debated right to work. For weeks, he had watched from the sidelines as right to work made its way through the laborious process of committee hearings, floor debates, smoke-filled conference rooms and back-room deals.

Now a heavy burden had been lifted from his shoulders and he was anxious to leave the unreal world of Baton Rouge with its thousands of political stargazers, bureaucrats, and hangers-on. People who worked at the capitol and other buildings connected to the boring, bloated government bureaucracy for fat paychecks and a couple of beers before returning home in the evening to get ready for the same routine the next day.

But most of all Leslie was lonesome for his wife Carolyn and his sons Scott and Mickey. He would see them later that morning, he thought, as he drove into the hotel parking lot.

John A. Curtis, the Prince Murat's night manager, had been struggling to stay awake during the early hours of the morning and was looking forward to the end of the long night shift. About 1:30 A.M., he went outside to break the monotony of the night, get some fresh air, and make sure everything was all right in the parking lots. He was standing in the driveway and waved at Leslie when he passed by.

Curtis said that a few minutes later he walked around the corner of the motel and was shocked when he saw Leslie lying face down in a pool of blood a short distance away from the back entrance. He ran across the parking lot and into the motel where he found a night security guard and yelled, "Call the police!"

Minutes later, at 1:57 A.M., three patrol cars, an unmarked detective car, and a K-9 corps officer arrived. The officers with their police dogs carefully checked the crime scene, but there was no one in the area. Within just a few minutes after the shooting, the assassins had vanished.

Curtis, who was visibly shaken by the killing, said he was standing in front of the motel when he heard the shotgun blast but thought it was the sound of fireworks from patrons of the Cahoots Night Club nearby who often became somewhat rowdy during the early morning hours. He added there was no one in the parking lot before Leslie arrived.

In a very bizarre twist, Leslie parked and locked his car right in front of the crack in the fence where the assassins were hiding in the shadows, and detectives said they were probably only four or five feet away from him at that time. There was a tree near the crack, and the officers said the assailant might have rested the weapon on the tree when he fired the fatal shot.

The crime scene investigators said Leslie was walking toward the motel entrance with his car keys in his right hand and his coat slung over his shoulder when the hidden assassins shot and killed him from a distance of about twenty feet. Detectives questioned all the residents in the wing of the Prince Murat where Leslie's room was located. One woman reported hearing the blast some time around 1:30 A.M.

After examining the crime scene, Detective Chris Schroeder said, "It was a well-planned homicide with very little physical evidence and no solid leads that would indicate who killed Leslie."

Another detective called it "a real professional hit."

Hill talked to medical examiner Hypolite Landry who said death came instantaneously from buckshot wounds to Leslie's heart and both lungs. According to his report, all sixteen of the OO buckshot pellets from the twelve-gauge shotgun—each with the killing capacity of a .32-caliber pistol—struck Leslie in the upper body.

Two of the individuals who attended the victory party at the Camelot Club informed the detectives they saw a mysterious stranger who seemed to be watching every move Leslie made during the party. The detectives believed he may have been serving as a lookout to alert the killers when Leslie left the party to return to his hotel. This really wasn't much of a lead but it was about all they had, so the detectives asked a police artist to work up a composite drawing of the stranger based on the description given to the investigators by the two guests at the Camelot.

Baton Rouge authorities later asked Shreveport police chief T. P. Kelley for pictures and information concerning certain individuals from North Louisiana who had criminal records. They apparently wanted to compare the pictures with the composite drawing. The chief had a grim look on his face when I walked into his office later that day and inquired about the pictures.

"Chief, I understand the Baton Rouge authorities sent you a composite drawing of a suspect in the Leslie murder and asked you to send them some pictures," I said. "Could you tell me whose pictures you sent to them?"

Kelley—ever the professional—shook his head and replied, "No."

He was a man of very few words and responded with "yes"

and "no" most of the time during my previous and subsequent interviews with him.

Anyway, I thought it was worth a try.

Since the right-to-work debate between the businessmen in the state and organized labor had been so acrimonious and there had been an earlier killing in Lake Charles, Louisiana, which was attributed to labor violence, Baton Rouge detectives at first thought Leslie's murder was related to labor unrest.

Organized labor had quite a history of violence in the state. I had read newspaper reports of Lester "Red" Lacour, business agent for the Carpenters Union Local 953 in Lake Charles, who had been arrested for his part in a mob attack at the Jupiter Chemical Company construction site only a few months earlier. During the attack, Lacour's mob killed a member of an independent union, and four others were injured when Lacour's men overran the construction site.[1] Authorities charged Lacour with criminal conspiracy and damage to property in the Jupiter case.

The Associated Press also reported, and our newspaper carried the story, that Lacour was linked to the so-called Ellender Bridge violence in which a mob attacked another labor site in the Lake Charles area and beat up a Mexican American crew. "Lacour was charged with conspiracy to commit aggravated assault and aggravated damage to property in connection with the bridge incident," the AP reported.

An assassin murdered Lacour in his home before his case ever went to trial. The killer found a way to get into his house late at night and shot him in the back of the head while he was asleep in bed.[2]

I don't believe Lake Charles authorities ever solved the Lacour murder.

Ken Grissom of the *Shreveport Journal* capital bureau raised several questions about Leslie's murder in an analysis entitled "Murderer Lurked Near Only Empty Parking Space." I read his article with great interest.[3] The *Journal* was our major competition in news coverage in Shreveport. Because the *Journal* was much smaller than the *Times* their reporters were quite aggressive—like the Avis Car Rental Company with the motto "We Try Harder." We had to fight them for every major news story we wrote.

Grissom thought it quite mysterious that the gunman was hiding in the shadows directly behind the only empty parking space in the 314-room hotel complex. "How could the gunman be sure the space would remain vacant and that Leslie would park there?" he asked.[4] According to Grissom, there were two questions the investigators were trying to answer: how did the assassin or assassins manage to hide behind the fence near the only vacant parking space and how did they escape unseen?[5] Since Leslie parked almost directly in front of the crack in the fence, the killer had a direct line of fire, he pointed out.[6]

Coincidence? Not likely.

According to Curtis, the night manager, conventioneers staying at the hotel had kept the parking lot full all week. Therefore, Grissom reasoned that the particular spot where Leslie parked would not have remained vacant unless an accomplice parked a car there and drove off just before Leslie arrived. So it was beginning to appear that the shooter or shooters had an accomplice.

I agreed with him.

"He could have been tipped off by a third person, acting as a spotter—stationed on a rooftop or following Leslie in a vehicle equipped with a CB radio—or he could have simply driven off as he saw Leslie's car enter the rear parking lot," Grissom stated.[7]

Shuler said the murder sent shock waves through the halls of the state capitol. The thought that some labor hit man may have killed Leslie made the legislators nervous. The representatives and senators and their aides and lobbyists walked quietly through the hallways of the beautiful building that Huey Long had built—its walls covered with marble imported from Italy—and spoke quietly to one another like a group of undertakers. Some wiped tears from their eyes.

Buddy Roemer, son of state commissioner of administration Charles Roemer and who later would become governor of the state, said that Leslie was like a member of his family.

"I went to get a sandwich with him at 8:00 P.M. last night," the younger Roemer said the day of the murder, "and he asked me to go to a party [at the Camelot], but I didn't go."

Early the next morning, he heard the terrible news that his good friend had been killed and it was a gut-wrenching experience for him. He knew he would miss his friend.

The American Federation of Labor and Congress of Industrial Organizations (AFL-CIO) Louisiana union leader Victor Bussie, who had been portrayed by Leslie's right-to-work television ads as a Svengali of the labor movement in Louisiana, said that his union members had nothing to do with Leslie's murder. (Svengali was the fictional hypnotist in George du Maurier's 1894 novel *Trilby*.)

Bussie was a tall, balding man who stood straight as an arrow. When he spoke, everyone listened. In a prepared statement, Bussie said:

> I was not acquainted with Mr. Leslie. . . . I know that I speak for the entire membership of the Louisiana AFL-CIO when I say that I am extremely dismayed by his death. I do not believe that his death had any connection with the issues before the legislature. Actually, few people knew that he had any part in the right-to-work fight. . . . Whatever was behind the tragic death, I hope and pray will be revealed soon and the person or persons responsible will be brought to justice. While we know nothing about these events, nevertheless, we offer our complete cooperation to all law enforcement people to help solve this case. All of us express our sincere condolences to the family.[8]

Law enforcement officers and those of us at the newspaper who knew Bussie came to the swift conclusion that it would have served no purpose for labor union officials, or some freelance union malcontent, to kill Leslie. That would have made it a vengeance killing and would have done more harm than good to the labor movement.

Presuming that vengeance was the motive for the killing, it seemed to me that Ed Steimel of the Louisiana Association of Business and Industry (LABI) or former state representative Jimmy Wilson of the Louisiana Right-to-Work Committee would have been more likely targets. Steimel for several years had fought against organized labor, which had strong and loyal support in both houses of the legislature, and certainly had become their nemesis.

Shuler told us that the chambers of the House of Representatives were quiet as Rep. George Holstead remembered Leslie and led the House of Representatives in prayer for his family.

"As the legislators said their own private prayers, the house chamber was hushed. Although not a word had been said before, there was a feeling of quiet tension and uncertainty running throughout the house," Shuler wrote.[9]

"I don't come here to eulogize Jim Leslie, although it is tragic that a young man striving to do a professional job had to have his life so sadly and suddenly terminated," Representative Holstead said as he wiped tears from underneath his glasses. "I want to express my condolences and I believe the condolences of this legislature to the family and loved ones of Jim Leslie."[10]

Representative Holstead also spoke in defense of the character and integrity of the leaders of the AFL-CIO.

"I have known Mr. Victor Bussie for many years and know him to be a kind and compassionate man," the representative said. "I respect him very sincerely, yet I very rarely agree with him philosophically. I feel very sad for Mr. Leslie's family and the leadership of the AFL-CIO."[11]

It was apparent to all of us that for Steimel and the members of LABI the right-to-work victory was bittersweet after Leslie was gunned down.

He also issued a statement:

It is indeed shocking to learn of Jim Leslie's assassination last night. He was a real artist and the most effective and creative media specialist I know. He was also a man who demonstrated the highest form of integrity. His death is a great loss to all of us and indeed a great loss to his profession.

We wish to express our most sincere condolences and sympathy to his family whose loss is far greater than ours.[12]

I was surprised when Steimel disclosed for the first time that during the right-to-work debate he had asked for police protection to escort him in and out of the senate chambers. He also said after the Leslie murder, state police officers had suggested that he not move about the chambers until things quieted down.

"I did that," he commented.

Steimel, living in the shadow of the Leslie murder, told our reporters that as a precautionary measure he had asked his family to leave home and stay with friends until more information on the murder came to light. Although he said he was not concerned for his own safety, some veiled threats by his opponents caused him concern for his family members. He did not elaborate on exactly what was said.

Governor Edwin Edwards, during a news conference where he signed the right-to-work legislation into law, called the killing a "terrible, brutal, unnecessary and senseless murder."[13] Edwards was the silver-haired "*Cajun* Fox" who, during his long political career, would serve four terms as governor of Louisiana, more than any other governor in the state's history.

The governor said Baton Rouge police officials awakened him at four o'clock in the morning and gave him the bad news about Leslie. He added that after the initial call, the officials continued to brief him every few hours.

Carl Liberto, the managing editor of the *Journal,* worked for Leslie in advertising and public relations prior to joining the newspaper and said that he was an all-around nice guy.

"Leslie was fun to work with and kidded around a lot," Liberto remarked. "He could get serious but otherwise he was the cop-on-the-corner type of guy."

According to Liberto, Leslie was "the man" in public relations and advertising in Shreveport.

"Jim was one of the smartest, nicest guys I ever dealt with in the PR business," Liberto said. "He was a real genius at conducting political campaigns, and if you had Jim backing you for any office, you were going to get elected."

Caddo Parish (County) sheriff Harold Terry, another Leslie client and close personal friend, was charged with the unhappy task of informing Leslie's wife, Carolyn, and his sons, Scott and Mickey, of the cold-blooded killing.

J. L. Wilson, a veteran *Times* reporter, told us that deputies said the sheriff was deeply moved by the loss of his friend and that his eyes were red from weeping as he left his office to go to the Leslie home on South Lakeshore Drive to give the family the bad news. Although we knew it was a terrible shock to the family, Sheriff Terry never commented on the personal way the Leslies handled the news of the tragedy as he tried to protect their privacy during the time of sadness.

McDaniel told all of us working on the Leslie story that no one, under any circumstances, was to call his widow for an interview during her time of bereavement. And we never did.

Leslie's body was returned to Shreveport on Friday night.

CHAPTER TWO

The Story

Both McDaniel and city editor Will McNutt appeared to be struggling to control their emotions that morning when they called J. L. Wilson and me into the office.

"J. L., I want you and Bill to write the story and keep us up to date on where we are," McDaniel said.

Neither of us said a word; we just nodded and left the office.

It's hard to describe the adrenaline rush I felt that morning as I began work on the biggest story of the year and maybe of the decade. I knew that our readers would want to know every detail of the Leslie murder. It was our job to give them all the facts, free of our personal feelings.

Wilson and I went to work and kept in touch with Hill and Shuler in the *Times* capital bureau in Baton Rouge, made several phone calls, ran down leads, and interviewed Police Chief Kelley, Dist. Atty. John Richardson, and others.

As we approached the deadline for the "Bulldog edition"— the early edition thrown together so fast it was as ugly as a bulldog—I was somewhat apprehensive when I realized I must call Commissioner of Public Safety George D'Artois for a statement. Although my mouth felt like it was filled with cotton and my hands were sweaty, I knew I had to try to interview him. The *Times* was not the commissioner's favorite newspaper, and I was not his favorite reporter. We had published a series of articles that raised questions about graft and corruption in his administration. We were also aware of his suspected ties to Carlos Marcello, the crime boss who ran the syndicate in New Orleans for some fifty years, and the rumors that they had discussed plans to bring organized crime to Shreveport.

George D'Artois was the most popular and effective commissioner of public safety in the history of Shreveport. He was the elected leader of the police, fire, and traffic engineering departments. (Courtesy LSUS Archives—Noel Memorial Library)

When he answered the phone, he was almost subdued as though frozen in time.

"Commissioner, this is Bill Keith at the *Times,* and I wanted to ask if you have any comment on the murder of Jim Leslie," I said.

He thought for a moment and replied, "I don't have anything to say to the *Shreveport Times,* nothing at all, nothing at all." Then he hung up the phone, and I heard a dial tone.

Captain Sam Burns, the director of the Organized Crime and Intelligence Division of the Shreveport Police Department, told me later that on the day after Leslie was murdered, he met with the commissioner, and they had a heated exchange.

"He started raising cane with me because the state attorney general's men, who were in Shreveport to investigate him, were riding patrol with some of our officers," Burns said. "When I mentioned the Leslie murder to him, all he said was, 'Yeah, murder is always a terrible thing. But when you stick your nose into organized labor, you'll get it cut off.'"[1]

"It can't be labor," Burns said.

The large, heavy-set commissioner, his face red with anger, came out from behind his desk like the Incredible Hulk, got in Burns' face and asked, "Just what are you trying to say?"

"I didn't respond but walked out of his office," Burns said.

At the time of the D'Artois-Burns encounter, Leslie's body was lying in state at the Marshall Street Chapel of the Rose-Neath Funeral Home in Shreveport.

On Saturday, the stories that J. L. and I wrote on the murder of Jim Leslie appeared in our paper. Although most of our readers had already heard the news via radio and television, our main article and the several sidebars provided in-depth coverage of the murder, the coroner's report, an update on the investigation, the response by Leslie's friends, and the atmosphere in the capitol in Baton Rouge after the killing.

Funeral services for Leslie were held on Monday at the First United Methodist Church. The Reverend Dr. D. L. Dykes, Leslie's pastor, conducted the service. There was an overflow crowd estimated at some five hundred who filled the chapel and the hallway of the church as the Reverend Dr. Dykes remembered Leslie as a man with the unusual characteristics of gentleness, a sense of responsibility, courage, respect and "early marks of greatness."[2]

"Those who knew him best say his greatest characteristic was gentleness," the Reverend Dykes said, adding that a person who knew him well once commented, "I never heard him say an unkind thing about any person, never a mean remark about anyone."[3]

The Reverend Dykes said that perhaps the greatest of all of Leslie's attributes was that "he was a good father, a good husband, and a good friend."

Burial was in Forest Park Cemetery. McDaniel, Leslie's close friend, was one of the pallbearers.

All those present at the funeral and all of us in the newsroom felt a deep sense of sympathy for his wife Carolyn Leslie and their sons. Moreover, everyone present at the Methodist church that day would always carry the memory of the two little boys, Scott and Mickey, standing at their mother's side near their father's casket, his final resting place. We all knew they were condemned for the rest of their lives to live with isolation, loneliness, and shattered dreams. However, Carolyn and her two boys were surrounded by loving friends and family who would help them through the terrible ordeal.

The words of St. Francis de Sales were so true the day Jim Leslie was laid to rest: "This is a perishing and mortal life, and death seizes the good among the bad, the young among the old."

Dying makes life important and, were I to write an ode to Jim Leslie, it would say, "He found the peace we all seek but few of us ever find."

Journal editor Stanley Tiner wrote a very moving eulogy to Leslie, and I greatly appreciated his insight into the matter.[4]

> He was the best that America produces. He did that which his conscience told him was right and never looked back, because the spirit that moved within him told him he had to do it that way. He was too strong, too good and too right, so they shot him down Friday. They shot-gunned him in the back and left him lying there dead in his own blood, the cowards did, because they couldn't stand his strength, his goodness, or his righteousness. Jim Leslie's murder was tragic and senseless and insane, but it speaks much about what plagues this nation. Those who speak up, who stand up for something, they get shot down; it happens every day, only this day it happened here and it is close and we feel the anguish. . . . His death shadows the mind of this state with intensely dark feelings, and the other issues of life in Louisiana suddenly seem inconsequential. . . . Only justice can answer Jim Leslie's death—and retribution. We must have both. Jim Leslie gave much of himself to the rest of us during his 38 years. We owe him the decency of justice today. The wit, and the laughter, and the smiles that Jim Leslie carried through life are gone now, but a part of him lives within those who loved him. That should give us the momentum to do the job that we know needs doing in Louisiana. The job that Jim Leslie never finished. It is our job now.

During the hectic weeks that followed, both McDaniel and I believed there was a more sinister explanation to Leslie's murder than a contract killing by a New Orleans hit man or a random killing by some disturbed union worker. Although the thought tormented us and we hesitated to think the unthinkable, both of us believed we knew who ordered Leslie's murder. If what we believed was true, the revelation would shake the foundations of law and order in Shreveport and bring the city to its knees. We were determined to find the truth come hell or occasional high water.

CHAPTER THREE

Prelude to Evil

On Friday evening, May 14, two months before Jim Leslie was murdered, the *Times* newsroom was filled with electric excitement. All of us sensed something big was going down. We saw the members of the enterprise team, which was composed of four of our best investigative reporters, going in and out of McDaniel's office. That was quite unusual for he seldom ever became personally involved in a story.

The team members conferred with each other, first at one desk, then at another, and worked together around a typewriter as the story took shape. None of us ever could have imagined the far-reaching implications of the story they were working on that evening and the big surprise they had planned for Commissioner D'Artois in Saturday morning's paper.

About 9:00 P.M., McDaniel called me into his office. I noticed he had a worried look on his face. He told me the team was getting ready to break a very damning story about D'Artois and that no one could predict how he would react.

"You need to get your family and get out of town," he told me. "Just get as far away as possible, and I don't even want to know where you are going. Call me in a few days, and if things have cooled down, I'll let you come back."

Although he didn't go into the specifics, he told me the story of how the commissioner had tried to pay Jim Leslie's advertising agency with a city check for personal work done for his reelection campaign. I later learned that Chief Kelley and Captain Burns were the ones who first told McDaniel about the unauthorized payment, and Leslie had confirmed it.

I did not know Jim Leslie that well. City editor McNutt had

introduced us and told me that Leslie once worked for our newspaper but resigned to form a public relations and advertising firm primarily to help political candidates get elected. He was a frequent visitor to our newsroom and often brought us news releases on behalf of his clients, but I never had the opportunity to visit with or interview him.

McDaniel did not tell me that he was also sending some of the enterprise team members to San Francisco to get them out of town for a few days. Although they would write numerous other stories that would raise questions about irregularities in D'Artois' police department, this story would be the most damning.

He explained that due to my high profile at city hall, where I worked every day covering my beat, and because I also had written articles about the commissioner, an act of retribution for the next day's story could be aimed at me.

I had learned never to question McDaniel, so I responded, "Okay, we'll leave tonight, but I'm broke and need some money."

McDaniel told his secretary, Elaine Troquille, to get me two hundred dollars.

I finished a couple of stories I was working on for the next morning's paper, then rushed home and told my wife we were leaving town. I explained what McDaniel had told me about the news story the enterprise team was going to break the next morning and that it could cause trouble.

"Where are we going?" she asked.

"I'm not sure, somewhere," I replied.

"Are we in danger?" she asked.

"I don't think so, but we're not going to take any chances," I said.

We packed a couple of suitcases and diapers for our little Lindsay, who was ten months old, and left Shreveport in a hurry.

As I drove east on Interstate 20 toward Monroe, Louisiana, I was tired but wired as all kinds of crazy thoughts ricocheted through my mind. Are we really in danger? I wondered. Will we be followed? Does McDaniel know something I don't know? Have there been threats against my life? The enterprise team was writing the big story that would expose the commissioner, so why did McDaniel want me out of town? I was just a heartbeat ahead of my worst fears. Only one thing was certain that night: I planned to have a long talk with the good Lord before the night was over.

I chain-smoked Marlboro cigarettes as we drove east on the interstate in our worn-out Oldsmobile. However, it was in better condition than our other car, the red, white, and blue Chevrolet Vega that puffed black and white smoke out the tail pipe.

Both of our children, Richard, ten, and Lindsay, were asleep in the back seat. As we traveled down the highway, I became a little paranoid. Every few seconds I would glance in my rear-view mirror to see if we were being followed. Then I would light another cigarette.

That night when I came to the realization that my life, which was sorely troubled by the shadows of my imagination, might be measured in days rather than decades, forever didn't seem very long any more.

"Bill, are you scared?" my wife asked me.

"No, I always turn this shade of pale when the sun goes down," I replied with a feeble attempt at humor.

Yeah, I was scared for only the dead are without fear. There are times when each of us is a prisoner of circumstances. However, there was no foreboding, just a whisper deep down in my soul that there is a promise of tomorrow and time never forgets.

Everything that transpired that night seemed so incongruous: the hard-hitting story about the commissioner that was to appear in the next morning's newspaper, the flight from Shreveport to a hiding place out of state, and, worst of all, wondering how the commissioner would react to the story.

When we arrived in Monroe about a hundred miles east of Shreveport, I pulled into the Howard Johnson's Motor Lodge and rented a room for the night. I unloaded our luggage and put the children to bed. My wife and I watched television for a couple of hours trying to relax, but it didn't help much.

About 2:00 A.M., I placed my .22 magnum pistol under my pillow and tried to sleep but was distracted by the slightest noise outside our room. Around daylight, after maybe two or three fitful hours of sleep, I unlocked the door to our room and went outside to find a newspaper box to get a copy of the *Times*. I was so nervous I could hardly get the quarter in the box. It finally opened, and I grabbed a copy. The headline above the fold screamed at me: "D'Artois Tried to Use City Funds to Pay Personal Bill."

At that point, I understood why McDaniel wanted me and the enterprise team to get out of town. The story was a strong exposé of the commissioner's questionable activities at city hall.

"Public Safety Commissioner George D'Artois tried to pay for $3,500 worth of personal political campaign expenses with a check drawn on the City of Shreveport on the basis of an invoice which had been altered, the *Shreveport Times* learned yesterday," the story said.[1]

The reporters wrote that the check was written on the City of Shreveport's general fund on November 11, 1974, to Jim Leslie & Associates, which originally had billed the commissioner for work performed during his most recent reelection campaign.

"The check was returned to Commissioner D'Artois by certified mail on Nov. 20, 1974," Leslie said. He also sent the commissioner a letter pointing out that the invoice mailed to him must have been confused with other invoices submitted by his agency for work done for the public safety department, the article pointed out.[2]

The enterprise team also reported that D'Artois tried a second time to pay Leslie with a city check.

"At a party several weeks later, Commissioner D'Artois handed me a sealed envelope," Leslie said. "When I got home that evening I opened the envelope and found that it contained the same check from the City of Shreveport."[3]

Leslie told the team that once again he consulted with his attorney and mailed the check back to D'Artois by certified mail, with an enclosed letter in which he wrote, "I will not accept this check."

They also learned that the original invoice he sent to D'Artois had been altered.

"Leslie's copy of the invoice form on Oct. 30, 1974, addressed to Commissioner George D'Artois, City Hall, Shreveport, Louisiana, bears a reference to 'Balance Due' on the left hand side of the invoice and the amount of $3,500 in the right hand column," the team reported. "A voucher in the city accounting office reflecting issuance of the check is accompanied by a photo static copy of the invoice but there are significant differences."[4]

They went on to explain: "Above the line on which D'Artois' name appears as addressee the invoice bears two additional lines, indicating that the invoice was addressed to Department of Public Safety, Police Community Relations, Storefront, Commissioner George W. D'Artois, City Hall, Shreveport, Louisiana."[5]

"And below the notation 'Balance Due' in the body of the invoice had been typed what appeared to be an itemized list of specific services for 'Storefront and Crime Prevention' campaigns . . . which had been [previously] handled by Leslie's agency."[6]

After reading the articles in the Saturday paper, we left Monroe and traveled only on back roads on our way to Natchez, Mississippi, where we would hide out for the next few days until McDaniel told us it was safe to return to Shreveport.

We checked into the Ramada Inn overlooking the majestic Mississippi River and during the time we were there never let our children out of our sight. We ate all of our meals at the Ramada restaurant or in our room. None of us went outside the hotel room at night. They were restless days and sleepless nights filled with anxiety and uncertainty. All night long I listened for sounds I didn't want to hear and endured the dirty tricks your mind plays on you as you try to deal with second-hand emotions. I also pondered the universal harmonies hidden beneath the chaotic experiences of my life.

My mind kept wandering back to Commissioner D'Artois and how far heroes fall. I was troubled by the feeling that the people of the erstwhile smooth-sailing City of Shreveport were about to witness the worst scandal in their history.

The family man in me wanted to protect my wife and children as I lived through every minute of the nightmare. However, the newsman in me wanted to be back in Shreveport in the middle of the investigation and help put those dreadful days to sleep forever.

When D'Artois read the story on that Saturday morning, he went into a rage, grabbed his Colt Python pistol and told his wife, Billie Claire, that he was going out to Lakeshore Drive to kill Jim Leslie.

Chief Kelley later explained to me exactly what happened that morning.[7]

Frantic, Billie Claire called Chief Kelley to ask him to stop her husband.

"George is on his way out to kill Jim Leslie!" she screamed into the phone.

Kelley's wife, Hazel, who answered the phone, informed her that the chief was already on his way downtown to the police station but that she would get in touch with him and give him the message.

Hazel Kelley called the chief and told him about the call from Billie Claire D'Artois. Chief Kelley keyed his hand radio and called the watch commander at the patrol desk.

"This is Kelley, get a car out to Jim Leslie's home at 6256 South Lakeshore Drive and see if you can find the commissioner!" Kelley said. "Get out there now. This is an emergency! And let me know if you find him."

A few minutes later, the watch commander called Kelley and said that a black and white had arrived at the Leslie home, but there was no sign of the commissioner. On his way to the station, Kelley ran across Fire Chief Dallas Greene, who was one of D'Artois' closest friends.

"We've got to find the commissioner and fast," he called out to Greene and then told him about the frantic phone call from Billie Claire.

Greene, who was a big, roly-poly man with a Conway Twitty haircut and a friendly smile, slid into the front seat of the police car. They drove up and down several streets, but there was no sign of the commissioner. They were on their way back to the police station when they spotted him driving aimlessly along a street in his gray Cadillac as though in a daze.

When they pulled him over to the side of the road, Greene asked him, "You all right, commissioner?"

D'Artois just nodded.

Both of the chiefs noticed he had a crazed look in his eyes and his face was so red they thought he was about to explode. They also remembered that he had experienced some heart trouble several months earlier.

"I think we should take him to Schumpert [Medical Center] and let them check him out," Greene said, fearful that his rage might trigger another heart attack.

"Yes, that's a good idea," Kelley said. He called Billie Claire and told her they had found the commissioner and that he was all right. "But we think we better put him in the hospital for observation."

"I'll meet you there," she said.

"George, we're going to take you to the hospital just to make sure everything is okay," Greene said.

"No, I want to go back to the office," D'Artois replied.

"Commissioner, let's go on to the hospital, and Billie Claire is going to meet us there," Green said.

They put the commissioner in the back seat and headed for Schumpert Medical Center on Margaret Place. Kelley called the station and asked the desk sergeant to send a patrolman to pick up the commissioner's Cadillac. During the ten-minute ride to the hospital, it was quiet in the car and nothing was said about the Leslie story that had appeared in the *Times*.

After the emergency room doctors examined him, they decided to admit him overnight so they could run some tests. However, he improved dramatically by midmorning and granted an interview in his hospital room to Wanda Warner of the *Journal*. It was apparent that he was eager to refute our story. Throughout the interview, he categorically denied the report that he had deliberately tried to use city funds to pay Jim Leslie for personal advertising expenses.[8]

"D'Artois said the check was drawn on the city's account because of a mistake in the accounting department," Warner reported. "He denied that he tried a second time to have Leslie cash the check."[9]

However, the *Times* had published pictures of both the original and the altered invoices on the front page of the newspaper that morning. The pictures were taken from records in the accounting department at city hall. There was no question that the invoice had been altered, just as the article reported. Suddenly the people of Shreveport began to realize the investigation of the commissioner was far more serious than any of them had imagined.

I later learned that when D'Artois arrived at the Leslie home no one was there. McDaniel had also advised Leslie to take his family and get out of town before the story broke.

Before Chief Kelley left the hospital that morning, D'Artois ordered him to station police officers at the door to his hospital room. Kelley called the watch commander and told him to adjust his duty roster to schedule his officers for the personal guard duty for the commissioner.

I never fully understood why the commissioner felt he needed around-the-clock protection in the hospital. I have thought since then that it could have been some kind of victim paranoia. Or he may have wanted to show everyone that he was still in command of the police force. He certainly was in no danger.

The next day, Sunday, May 16, the people of Shreveport awakened to a surprise that shook the foundations of their confidence in law and order in the city, as our newspaper called for D'Artois to step down as commissioner of public safety.

A page-one headline read, "Times Urges D'Artois Be Relieved of Duties." The front-page article presented a brief summary of the editorial that appeared on the editorial page.

Jim Montgomery, the newspaper's editorial writer, stated: "*The Shreveport Times* feels that George D'Artois should be relieved of his duties as commissioner of public safety and, further, that he should be denied access to the records and operations of the office and the department so that a thorough investigation of his activities can be conducted."[10]

The editorial said it would be difficult for the mayor and city council to conduct a credible investigation as long as the commissioner continued to be in charge of the public safety department.

"As one Identification Division employee so aptly expressed it in a conversation with the *Times* last week, 'If the commissioner tells us to take something out of the records—we can't ask 'Why, commissioner?' He's the boss.'"[11]

The editorial went on to explain various other reasons why the commissioner should be relieved of his duties.[12]

With Mayor Calhoun Allen's announcement Thursday [before D'Artois entered the hospital] that he would call the City Council into special session Monday to initiate a council probe, there seemed at first to be reason for hope, but it soon became apparent that Mr. D'Artois was attempting to engineer his own investigation into his own activities.

Mayor Allen removed both Chief of Police T. P. Kelley and Chief of Detectives J. K. Lanigan from an internal criminal investigation that was already in progress, skipped over a number of other ranking department officials and detectives, and appointed Lt. Dan Coker to head the special investigation, with detectives Bill Burson and Bill Strange completing the team.

Yet during the day on Thursday the three men appointed to the investigation met on several occasions in private with Mr. D'Artois—the man they were supposed to be investigating—and it was Mr. D'Artois who informed them they were to be assigned to the investigation. Also, following a lengthy meeting with Mayor Allen, Lt. Coker went immediately to Mr. D'Artois' office.

No reasonable investigation can be conducted in this atmosphere and this atmosphere will most likely continue so long as Mr. D'Artois remains in office during the investigation.

We question the propriety of Mayor Allen taking people off a criminal investigation already in progress—an investigation that was almost concluded—and we certainly doubt the propriety of replacing the chief of police and chief of detectives with low-ranking members of the department. . . .

Mr. Kelley and Mr. Lanigan are highly trained professionals—men of experience, expertise and integrity—who, above all other people in the department should be in command of an investigation of this magnitude. They should be put back on the investigation at once.

Montgomery also pointed out that D'Artois had suffered a serious heart attack several months earlier and suggested that it would be best for him personally if he were to be removed from the "difficult and demanding atmosphere which naturally accompanies such an investigation."

"Meanwhile, evidence of Mr. D'Artois' questionable activities continues to pile up," the editorial continued. "It is the responsibility of the City Council to see that a thorough, uncompromising investigation—one not controlled by the official who is being investigated—is conducted. It is the responsibility of the City Council to relieve Mr. D'Artois of his duties and deny him access to the office for the duration of the investigation."[13]

There were two other hard-hitting investigative stories by the enterprise team about D'Artois in the Sunday *Times* that revealed his unquestioned authority and abuse of power. One, written by Lynn Stewart, presented documented evidence that D'Artois had granted liquor permits to several people who did not meet the requirements since they had either felony arrest records or direct ties to criminals. Another story by Margaret Martin reported that D'Artois was cited in a federal court case as being at the Oak Lawn Racetrack in Hot Springs, Arkansas, during early March of 1975 with a man by the name of Fred Box who had been arrested several times on various charges.

Stewart carefully documented instances where the commissioner gave preferential treatment to some of his old friends and cronies seeking liquor licenses in the city. The headline read, "Preferential Treatment Confirmed by Records." "A *Times* review of applications for liquor permits showed that in at least eight instances D'Artois has directed his subordinates to grant permits to persons who have not met all requirements for those permits," the article reported.[14]

D'Artois granted exceptions and approved liquor licenses for Joe Anthony Catanese who had previously been arrested for theft and was convicted of bank robbery and receiving stolen goods; Charlie Hopkins, whose arrests included charges of operating a gambling game, letting a disorderly house, and selling beer and whiskey without a license; and Joe S. Cush, who had been arrested for illegal gambling, drunkenness, and the sale of liquor on Sunday.[15]

Louisiana law was quite specific concerning liquor license permits, but D'Artois apparently had been reading the law like the funny papers. It was apparent he harbored a blatant disregard for state laws and was determined to make his own laws.

According to Stewart's article, a typical notation on the permit might say, "There is no certificate of occupancy. . . . The commissioner brought him back and said it was okay." The notation was written in red ink on the application.[16] Louisiana law required the certificate of occupancy.

There were similar notations on the application submitted by Joe Anthony Catanese. Although state law prohibited convicted felons from receiving a liquor license, D'Artois personally approved his license.[17]

The headline for Martin's story read, "D'Artois Is Figure in Race Track Suit." The article, filed by Martin from Hot Springs, Arkansas, revealed that D'Artois had been present at the Oaklawn Race Track in Hot Springs when his close friend Henry Floyd "Red" Box was ejected from the track and arrested. Box, who had several previous arrests, was considered an undesirable by track officials. The charges later were dropped.[18]

Box, the owner of a Shreveport amusement center, once stated that his hobby was "betting and wagering on sporting events, principally football games and horse races."

"On Oct. 14, 1975, Box filed a suit against Oaklawn saying he had been falsely, illegally and maliciously placed under arrest and manhandled by guards. . . . Commissioner D'Artois was a witness, according to records in the case."[19]

Martin's story listed the names of the people with Box when he was arrested. They were D'Artois and his wife Billie Claire, Vito Cefalu, and Patsy Dunbar, all of Shreveport.

Hot Springs police authorities, Assistant Chief of Police Marvin Owen and Lt. Bob Griffith, said they had seen Commissioner D'Artois with Box at Oaklawn on several occasions.[20]

"Both Owen and Griffith said that D'Artois introduced himself as the public safety commissioner from Shreveport when he came down to the security office with Box the day he was arrested," Martin wrote. "And they said the commissioner spoke favorably to them about Box."[21]

Martin researched D'Artois' travel records to discover whether several chartered airplane flights were connected to Hot Springs racetrack visits by Box.[22] She learned that on March 10 of that year, the date when Box was arrested at the track, D'Artois chartered a plane to Hot Springs.

Also, on March 17, he chartered a plane to Little Rock. Box was scheduled to appear in court in Hot Springs, about fifty miles from Little Rock, the next day. Although the evidence was circumstantial, it did raise questions about the commissioner's charter air travel.

In essence, it appeared that the taxpayers were paying thousands of dollars for charter flights to take the commissioner's friends back and forth from Shreveport to Hot Springs for gambling and court appearances. The charter flights, of course, were paid with city/taxpayer funds. The city's finance office didn't have a clue concerning the nature of the flights and never questioned the commissioner about them.

It was a real eye-opener to those of us at the newspaper and to the people of Shreveport when we learned that the powerful commissioner was running around with a bunch of cronies who had police records and lived right on the edge of the law.

After the investigative reports on the attempted felony theft of city funds, the stories by Stewart and Martin, and the hard-hitting editorial in Sunday's edition, our readers realized they were seeing the dark side of law enforcement and that Shreveport had become a city in search of its soul.

I didn't want to stay in Mississippi much longer. It's tough for a reporter to stand on the sidelines and watch historic events unfold. So, on Tuesday, I called McDaniel, and he informed me that after the Leslie story broke on Saturday, the commissioner was so upset he had to be hospitalized.

"He's still in the hospital so I believe it's safe for you to come on back now," he said.

As we made the long drive back to Shreveport, I wondered if our leaving town had been a false alarm and "much ado about nothing."

We arrived back in Shreveport on Tuesday night, and the next day, when I went to city hall to follow up on several stories related to the investigation, I heard some disturbing news. I met Captain Burns in the hall, and he said, "Bill, George [D'Artois] has been talking to some shady characters in his hospital room including Cliff Guevara."

Although I had never met Guevara, I knew his brother John who was a police lieutenant and a real stand-up guy. However, Burns said that Cliff Guevara had a police record of several arrests and was the proprietor of a dive called the Pyramid Club out on Jewella Avenue.

"We don't know why he wanted to talk to Guevara," Burns said. "But some of the guys are taking bets on who is going to be killed, you or Jim Leslie."

Then he smiled, but I didn't think it was funny. The thought sent cold chills up and down my spine and caused me to break out in a sweat. I was so shaken up I had to step outside to take a long smoke, get some fresh air and a grip on myself.

Burns also told me that during the past few days, he had been receiving calls from D'Artois' secretary saying the commissioner wanted to see him at the hospital.[23]

"I was scared to go but finally went," Burns said. "When I entered the room, he started defending himself. He said, 'My side of the story hasn't come up to bat yet.'"

The police captain told me the only comment the commissioner made about the most recent *Times* story was that "Jim Leslie is a no good SOB." He further explained to me that through the years the commissioner had done many good things for the police department, "but now he was tearing it all down."

The captain added, "Bill, I know George would have you killed if he had a chance."

After I heard that, I asked my colleague J. L. Wilson to loan me his double-barreled shotgun and, from that day forward, I carried it with me in my car everywhere I went.

Several weeks later, Guevara told investigators that D'Artois had asked him to kill Leslie and Burns.

"Those were dangerous times," Burns told me years later. "When I parked and locked my car, I put tape on the hood and on the doors to make sure I would know if anyone had been tampering with it."

About that time there was another dramatic scenario that played out and revealed the depth of the commissioner's treachery and intrigue.

The *Times* and the *Journal* both were located in the *Times'* building at 222 Lake Street in the business district of downtown Shreveport. The newspapers had formed the Newspaper Production Company, which handled all advertising, production, and printing for both papers. It was a sweetheart deal that earned a lot of money for the owners of the papers.

They also shared a common telephone switchboard and employed half a dozen operators to handle all the incoming and outgoing calls. I was friendly with the operators, mostly elderly women, and often went to the switchboard to laugh and joke with them and thank them for helping me, particularly when I faced a deadline and needed to contact a source that could be anywhere in the United States. The operators always went the so-called "extra mile."

Maude was one of the older operators. She was a wonderful woman but had a problem—she liked to eavesdrop on the reporters' calls. McDaniel had warned Maude and the others that if they were caught listening in on private conversations they would be fired. Nevertheless, Maude continued listening to and enjoying the various conversations, particularly during the D'Artois investigation by the *Times*.

She also listened to conversations from the *Journal* newsroom. One day, she overheard a plot to discredit me by planting drugs in my car to make it appear that I was a drug dealer. It scared her, and she wanted to tell me about it but knew that if she did she would lose her job.

Another one of the switchboard operators, whose name I can't remember, came to me and said that Maude had heard something important but couldn't tell me because she would lose her job. I later learned that Maude would have been willing to give up her job to protect me.

I went to McDaniel and told him what Maude had said and that she knew she had violated his order not to listen in on conversations. He said he would make an exception in Maude's case. She told me the following story.

Officer Sam Bolen was a narcotics officer in the Shreveport Police Department. His wife, Diane Attaway Bolen, was a reporter in the *Journal* newsroom and the daughter of Douglas Attaway, the owner. One afternoon, Bolen called his wife, and Maude overheard him say that D'Artois had ordered one of the men in the narcotics division, he did not give his name, to plant drugs in my car and arrest me. Then, he said, the commissioner could say that at least one of the reporters writing unfavorable stories about him was a drug dealer. There was no indication Bolen was involved in any way.

Maude probably saved me from a lot of embarrassment that day. I later thought how incongruous it would have been for me to be arrested on drug charges since I had never even smoked a marijuana cigarette or used drugs of any kind.

After my conversation with Maude, I decided to tell the story to one of my friends with the FBI in the federal building. I never ever enjoyed going to their office. The agents always kept the doors locked and were so suspicious and secretive they would look at me through a peephole in the door.

"What is your name?" an unseen agent would ask from behind the door.

"My name is Bill Keith, I'm with the *Times*," I replied.

"What is the nature of your business?" he asked.

"I want to talk to agent Billy Thomas."

"Concerning what issue?"

By then, my patience was wearing a little thin as I said, "It's related to the George D'Artois investigation."

"Hold on."

I never understood why the agents were so mysterious. They certainly were not incognito for I could spot them a block away on a downtown street. They always wore trench coats, sunglasses, and hats pulled down low in front. And they all looked just alike.

A few minutes later, Thomas, a personable fellow who had become a good friend, opened the door. I told him about the plot to plant drugs in my car.

Thomas stated he would really like to help me. He was well aware of our investigation of the commissioner, but since it was not a federal issue, there wasn't much he and the other agents could do. He promised to keep an eye on the situation and would be available to testify as to what I had told him if the commissioner followed through with the plan to plant the drugs and arrest me.

When I arrived back at city hall that afternoon, I shared the information about the plot with Chief Kelley, Chief of Detectives Kenneth Lanigan, and Judge Dan Sawyer.

"They're talking about planting drugs in my car, and I hope they do," I said, "because the FBI will be watching my car."

Then I spread the same story all around the police department and knew that some snitch would inform D'Artois. I stretched the truth on that one since the guys at the FBI did not really promise to watch my car, but it worked. D'Artois abandoned the idea.

CHAPTER FOUR

A Secret Meeting

The epic drama of the rise and fall of Commissioner George
D'Artois actually began to unfold in late March of 1976 during a
secret meeting at the *Shreveport Times,* four months before Jim
Leslie was murdered. That meeting set the stage for the newspaper's
exposé of the commissioner and his cavalier attitude toward and
reckless abandon of law and order in the City of Shreveport.

After the harsh winter of 1975-76, spring came and brought with
it the beautiful azaleas, dogwood, and redbud trees to the streets of
Shreveport along with warm days and cool nights.

On one of those early spring days, Police Chief Kelley and Captain
Burns drove away from the police station on Murphy Street in an
unmarked police car and headed downtown toward the offices of
the *Shreveport Times* at 222 Lake Street. They were going to the
newspaper for a clandestine meeting with Howard Bronson, the
publisher, and McDaniel, the editor.[1]

The veteran police officers knew they were on a dangerous
mission and what they planned to tell the men at the newspaper
could cost them their jobs, or their lives. They also were aware that
if their boss, Commissioner D'Artois, were to find out about their
secret meeting, he would consider it a challenge to his tyrannical
rule in the police department and would seek revenge.[2]

Chief Kelley, a giant of a man with a gentle smile and soft voice,
had been transferred to Louisiana in the late 1960s, where he was
named special agent for the Shreveport office of the FBI. He had
served in the bureau for thirty-four years before he retired in 1971.
Later he became the city's chief of police.

"The FBI was an important part of my life all those years," he
told me during a lengthy interview in April of 2006. Throughout

53

his career as a G-man, he often worked with the legendary J. Edgar Hoover, longtime director of the bureau.

Shreveport mayor Calhoun Allen had followed Kelley's career with the FBI and knew he was a man of integrity, exactly the kind of man the city needed to run the police department.

"The mayor and Fire Chief Dallas Greene came to my office and asked me to come over to city hall and become the chief of police," Kelley said. "A few days later, I accepted the job."[3]

Mayor Allen had heard rumors of D'Artois' excessive gambling and suspected unlawful activities. He believed bringing Kelley to the police force might allay some of the doubts certain people in the city had about the commissioner. The mayor wasn't sure the rumors were true, but he feared that since there was so much smoke, and so much talk, there must be a fire somewhere.

Captain Burns, who had whiskers beyond the shadow stage but too short for a beard, was a classic tough guy with a perpetual grin on his rugged face. He was in charge of Shreveport's Organized Crime and Intelligence Division, which kept a watchful eye on vice and crime in the city. Although he was slight in stature and had a pinch of gypsy, humor, and élan, he acted as if he was bulletproof and ten-foot tall. A sixteen-year veteran, he had the reputation of being a tough but fair cop and was one of the best detectives ever to serve on the Shreveport police force.

Kelley was his boss and friend, and he knew Burns was a man he could trust.

The captain also had great respect for Kelley and once told me, "The chief was probably the most honest man I've ever known."[4]

Their friendship would prove to be important for both of them. They watched out for each other as they faced the dangerous days ahead and witnessed the underbelly of the beast of lawlessness right in the high office of the police department.

They had spent hours in secret, discussing the dark side of the department and the mystery, intrigue, and suspected corruption on the part of the commissioner. But since he was their boss and ruled the department with an iron fist, they felt there was very little they could do about it. They decided to ask the men at the newspaper for help but agreed the meeting must be kept secret.

Bronson and McDaniel welcomed the two officers to the newspaper and escorted them into the conference room, a place of privacy away from the busy newsroom filled with reporters working on stories and trying to meet a deadline for the next day's newspaper, which had the largest daily circulation in North Louisiana.

Bronson, a tall, athletic man, was the son of the far-famed Bill Bronson, the former courageous editor and publisher of the *Times*. His father was a staunch advocate of good government and was one of the toughest crusading newspapermen in America. He was also the archenemy of the Ku Klux Klan, which was active in Northwest Louisiana.

However, Howard Bronson, who was as handsome as any movie star in Hollywood, never developed the fire of the crusading newspaperman like his father. He was more involved in the management affairs of the newspaper.

McDaniel, a much shorter man with a gruff appearance, was serious to a fault and seldom ever smiled. Like his predecessor, he ruled the newspaper with an iron will and nerves of steel and made it clear to all of us who worked for him that we would do things his way or hit the highway. But he was fair. There were times when I was catching a lot of flak from the politicians at city hall—even threats of bodily harm because of my investigations. I was glad McDaniel was in my corner for he was so wise and never backed down to anyone.

Kelley and McDaniel were close friends, and the chief knew that McDaniel, like Captain Burns, was a man he could trust. They both were deacons in the Baptist church and often spoke on the phone or visited with each other over lunch.

None of the men in the conference room that afternoon had any idea of the far-reaching implications of their meeting. However, what transpired there that day would change their lives, and the lives of the people of Shreveport, forever.

During my interviews with Kelley and Burns in March and April of 2006, they related the following details of their meeting at the newspaper to me.

Kelley was the first to speak.

"We have a serious matter to discuss with you this afternoon," Kelley stated. "A very serious matter."

"We're here to listen," McDaniel said.

Kelley then explained that Commissioner D'Artois had been spending a lot of money betting on the ponies and losing his shirt at the local Louisiana Downs Racetrack, and they feared he had developed a serious gambling problem.

"He has chartered private airplanes, at the taxpayers' expense, to go to the Oaklawn Park Racetrack in Hot Springs, Arkansas, and also to Las Vegas, to gamble," Kelley informed them.

A later investigation by the *Times* enterprise team revealed just how serious his gambling problem had become. I checked the phone records in the police department and discovered that he even placed bets with a gambler in Las Vegas by the name of Val Roulette using a city phone during working hours.

Suddenly there was an eerie hush in the conference room as Bronson and McDaniel stared back and forth at the police chief and then at one another. Kelley continued by saying he believed D'Artois was paying for his excessive gambling habit with payoffs from several shadowy men who were running illegal gambling games throughout the city, bar and nightclub owners who were allowed to stay open all night, and from convenience stores in certain areas of the city that sold liquor on Sunday under D'Artois' protection.

Captain Burns reminded the newspapermen that at the time gambling was a violation of city ordinance and state law and, not being regulated, often resulted in fights with knives and straight razors and shootings, particularly in the black bars and nightclubs on Saturday nights. Hence, the illegal games created serious problems for law enforcement in the city. It required more time for

Burns and his detectives to investigate a murder case or a serious assault with a straight razor than to break up a gambling game.

The officers pointed out that there was a more serious problem than a dice or poker game in vacant or rented houses in certain areas of the city or in the back of a local bar or nightclub. By taking payoffs to allow these games to run, the commissioner was violating his oath to uphold the law and was undermining the work of his own police officers through selective enforcement of those laws. For this reason, they believed the top law enforcement officer in the city was contributing to lawlessness throughout the city.

"My men know what's going on and that it's illegal, but the commissioner won't let us bust them," Burns said. "Finally, I asked Chief Kelley to order me to break up the games. He did, and it made George [D'Artois] mad, but I told him the chief had ordered it."[5]

"George was furious when the officers raided the gambling games," Kelley added. "After that he was very cool toward me but he couldn't do anything about it."

The newsmen were shocked when they heard the sordid details of D'Artois' alleged web of deceit. McDaniel, who never wasted time on small talk and never missed a detail, had harbored some suspicions about the commissioner ever since Caddo Parish sheriff Jimmy Goslin and his deputies confiscated and destroyed the illegal payoff pinball gambling machines in the city. He had wondered why D'Artois had allowed the gambling to continue and spread throughout the city and why his officers had not shut down the illegal operations that reportedly netted some two million dollars a year. McDaniel also had other reasons to be concerned about the commissioner.

Charlotte Burrows, one of the *Times'* top reporters, once overheard a conversation between D'Artois and a gambler. It was after business hours at city hall, and she went by the commissioner's office to ask some questions related to a story she was writing. Both the receptionist and secretary had gone for the day. Realizing he had someone in his office, she sat down in the outer office and waited to see him. As she waited, she overheard their conversation, and it was apparent that they were discussing an illegal gambling operation.

At first, their dialogue startled her, then it frightened her. If they knew she had overheard their conversation, she could be in danger. Therefore, she quietly left the office, undetected, and returned to the newspaper's headquarters. She told McDaniel what she had heard but never probed further into the matter.[6]

Both McDaniel and Bronson realized D'Artois was a very popular public figure in Shreveport. He had been successful in keeping racial violence from erupting in the city in the turbulent 1960s and was responsible for developing the finest police and fire departments in the state. McDaniel said a prominent businessman once told him, "We know George takes some money on the side, but we ain't got no nigger problems in Shreveport."

During the meeting, Burns explained to the men exactly how D'Artois provided protection for the stores selling liquor on Sundays.

"'If you go out to stop Sunday liquor sales, let me know first,'" Burns said D'Artois told him. "Then the commissioner would inform the stores that they were about to be raided, and they would shut down their operation. When my boys got there, everything was shut down."[7]

Kelley and Burns had some other theories about how the commissioner probably was paying for his gambling addiction.

"D'Artois may also be using the money from the police informant's fund, money set aside to pay for information about drug trafficking and other criminal activities in the city," Kelley explained, adding that it would be a simple matter to determine if, in fact, D'Artois was using those funds for his gambling.[8] "There should be records in the finance office at city hall of all checks given to D'Artois to pay the informants. And he should have receipts for the money paid to each informant."

However, Kelley was convinced the commissioner did not have any receipts and through the years had stolen tens of thousands of dollars from the informant's fund to feed his gambling habit and his penchant for living the so-called "good life" that only money, and plenty of it, can provide.

Burns further stated that the commissioner even had his own bagman, a black police officer by the name of Leemon Brown, who made the rounds with a briefcase each Monday morning to pick up the payoff money from bars, night clubs, and convenience store owners.[9] Brown was an enforcer with the reputation of being a very dangerous man, and people in the black community were afraid of him.

The first time I ever saw Detective Brown he looked like a "stud" from the hood. He wore shoes with three-inch heels and a hat and fancy suit from one of the high-fashion clothiers in downtown Shreveport that catered primarily to black men. I thought he looked like the hottest thing since chili pepper.

Women who wanted children in order to draw a welfare check sometimes paid men known as "studs" to impregnate them. After the children were born, they often gave the studs a percentage of the checks. The studs made a lot of money, wore fancy clothes, and drove Cadillacs.

Captain Burns told Bronson and McDaniel that the commissioner also performed special favors for bar and nightclub owners.

"He allows some of them to stay open all night, and they pay him for the privilege," Burns said.

If one of the owners refused to pay, D'Artois would dispatch a police patrol car to the club and order the officer to park right at the front door with the police car lights flashing. A police officer explained to me that the patrons were reluctant to enter the club with the lights flashing, and soon the owner would cave in and start paying D'Artois again.

Neither of the newspapermen was prepared to hear what Kelley told them next. He said things were so bad in the police department that he was thinking about resigning from his office as chief of police.[10]

"I'm concerned that I might be incriminated in what the commissioner is doing," he said.

McDaniel stared at Kelley through horn-rimmed glasses and said, "Oh, no you're not! We're going to help you."

Burns, who knew of the influence D'Artois had over the

businessmen in the city and possibly with some of the owners of the newspaper, stated, "Mr. McDaniel, if you don't follow through on this, you'll be leaving me and the chief out on a limb."[11]

"We'll follow through. You can count on it," McDaniel replied.

Before the policemen left the newspaper office that afternoon, Kelley also told McDaniel that D'Artois tried to pay local advertising man Jim Leslie with a city check for a personal campaign reelection debt.

McDaniel said he would look into it.

Chief Kelley was encouraged after the meeting and decided to continue as chief of police and do his best to help expose the wrongdoing and malfeasance in the department. Captain Burns promised to help him.

As they returned to the police department that March afternoon, they knew they faced an uncertain future. The commissioner was a powerful and dangerous man, so they agreed to take certain precautions to protect one another.

CHAPTER FIVE

Law and Disorder

After the secret meeting in late March of 1976, McDaniel decided to follow up on the information given to him and Bronson by Chief Kelly and Captain Burns. However, the thought of an investigation of the most powerful lawman in northwest Louisiana troubled him. He knew that Commissioner D'Artois was cunning and a master at manipulating people. He would be a formidable adversary.

There was also another consideration. The newspaper was an integral part of the business establishment in the city. He realized that, in a sense, a challenge of the powerful police commissioner would be a challenge of the establishment. He even wondered how the owners of the newspaper and other business leaders might react to the investigation of a law-and-order icon in the city. He had heard rumors that D'Artois had done special favors for some of the owners' children and that troubled him.

I can imagine these many years later that McDaniel felt like he and the newspaper would be sailing into uncharted waters, and he didn't want to sink the ship.

All weekend he wrestled with the most important decision of his newspaper career. He finally came to the conclusion that he must keep faith with the police officers who had the courage to tell him about what they believed to be deceitfulness and duplicity in high places in city government.

He spoke with various members on the newspaper's board and told me that Pat Ewing Kendrick, one of the principal owners, encouraged him to investigate the allegations. The others agreed. McDaniel also shared his plans with managing editor Allan Lazarus, probably the most knowledgeable newspaperman in Louisiana, and city editor Will McNutt, an old pro who was responsible for all the local news coverage in the city. He knew he could count on their counsel and support.

Then he met with the enterprise team, which included four of the best investigative journalists at the newspaper, and instructed them to follow up on the information he had received concerning the commissioner's use of confidential informant's funds. That would be their first assignment but not the last. The four veteran reporters were Lynn Stewart, an award-winning journalist who was the team editor; Charlotte Burrows, the assistant managing editor of the newspaper and a star reporter; Margaret Martin, another award-winning reporter; and Orland Dodson, who was probably the best writer at the paper.

McDaniel's instructions were quite clear: determine how much money the commissioner received from the fund, how the money was used, and if there was any proof that the funds were indeed paid to informants. He insisted that the team's new assignment would be a top-priority investigation.

"And I want to keep it top secret, even from the reporters in the newsroom," he said.

He briefed them on a broad spectrum of alleged criminal activity in the police department, including the allegations of payoffs to the commissioner from bar and nightclub owners and gambling games that were out of control and often resulted in violence. He shared with them the information about the commissioner's attempt to pay Jim Leslie with a city check for work the advertising man had done for his personal reelection campaign. It was clear to the team that they had their work cut out for them and that it would take weeks and even months to investigate all the allegations that were made by Chief Kelley and Captain Burns.

Although I was the city hall reporter and had experienced some success in my own investigation of irregularities in the city's public utilities department a year earlier, McDaniel never told me about the D'Artois investigation. I didn't have a clue as to what was happening. Several times, I noticed the team members in the city hall office of the finance commissioner, George Burton. I was curious but presumed they had a good reason for being there.

One day, I met Margaret Martin in the hall outside Commissioner Burton's office.

"What's going on in the finance office?" I asked, thinking perhaps it was something I should know about.

"We're just checking some records," Martin replied with a smile.

As the deadline for publishing the first investigative report drew near, the enterprise team members knew they had to interview Commissioner D'Artois to give him a chance to respond to their story. They approached the interview with some trepidation but asked him several pointed questions about the large amounts of money he was drawing from the finance office, ostensibly to pay police informants, and how the money was used.

Stewart said the commissioner explained in a rather matter-of-fact way that the money was used in special investigations and for information from confidential informants concerning organized crime and narcotics traffic in the city.[1] She added that if he was at all concerned about their questions, he was careful not to reveal that concern to them. Rather, he was arrogant toward the three young women reporters. However, his demeanor began to change when they asked him if he had receipts for when and to whom the funds were disbursed. He handed them a manila envelope containing some receipts, copies of offense reports, and scraps of paper. Yet, after careful examination, they saw there were no valid receipts confirming the funds were actually paid to informants.

"He looked like a man who suddenly realized he had been caught," Stewart said.

After the interview, he called the newspaper and asked for an appointment with Bronson. According to Bronson, the commissioner told him that he had done nothing wrong and that a story about his alleged misuse of funds would be damaging to both him and his family.

"He asked me to stop the story," Bronson said in an interview in April of 2006. "I told him that I couldn't interfere with what the newsroom was doing."[2]

Bronson never heard from the commissioner again.

On Friday, April 23, I sensed the enterprise team members were working on a very important story.

"You got any idea what they're doing?" I asked J. L. Wilson whose desk was adjacent to mine.

"Not a clue," he replied.

The team members went in and out of McDaniel's office several times. I saw them conferring with one another in serious conversation at their desks and looking over one another's shoulders as they typed their story. In addition, McDaniel appeared to be uptight and more nervous than usual and, of course, later I understood why.

On Sunday morning, April 25, the newspaper broke the story with the headline "Misuse of City Funds Found by *Times* Survey." The essence of the story was that Commissioner D'Artois was receiving large sums of money to pay police informants with only a vague indication of how the money was used. They pointed out that in each case the funds were requested by the commissioner and approved without question by the finance office.

"They include 43 payments totaling $17,300 paid in the last 15 months to Commissioner of Public Safety George D'Artois personally."[3]

The enterprise team reported that the only information on file in the finance office to explain how the funds were being allocated were brief letters from D'Artois noting they were "for obtaining evidence and information from informants on organized crime cases."[4] Although the various divisions in the police department were required to keep meticulous records of their expenditures, D'Artois could not account for how he used the money paid to him. During the enterprise team's interview with the commissioner, he said only that the amount he received in 1975 and the early part of 1976 was "whatever the finance department says it is."[5] When the team members interviewed Chief Kelley, he said he did not know the purpose of the payments issued to D'Artois.

"You'll have to ask him about that," was Kelley's response.

Kelley, determined not to let the commissioner know he had

told the newspaper about the suspected misuse of the informant's fund, acknowledged the commissioner could be working on something confidential and therefore would be reluctant to share the information with the news media.

"He would not be compelled to tell me about it," Kelley said.[6]

Kelley told the reporters it was a common practice for his officers to receive funds for criminal investigations. The informants, though some of them were rather shadowy characters who lived on the edge of the law, often helped police officers arrest drug dealers, break up theft rings, and capture armed-robbery suspects. But he carefully monitored those cases and had records to document all expenditures.

Meanwhile, Finance Commissioner Burton said he was aware of the payments to D'Artois.

"They are for informant's fees, I'm told," he stated.[7]

In that Sunday's edition, the *Times* also carried a chart, which listed each of the checks issued to D'Artois from January 1975 to March of 1976.

The reporters had worked for a month verifying all their facts and checking and rechecking every detail before they broke the original story. Although the story did not accuse the commissioner of stealing money from the informant's fund, the presumption was that he was taking nearly a thousand dollars a month out of the fund for personal use. We later learned that was only the tip of the iceberg.

When I read the Sunday paper before going to church, I remembered something that had happened the first day I met D'Artois. A few days after I went to work for the newspaper in April of 1975, Will McNutt asked my fellow reporter J. L. Wilson to assist with my orientation.

"Take Bill over to city hall and introduce him to the mayor, the commissioners, and other city officials. Help him get acquainted," McNutt said.

We had to go through the offices of two secretaries to get to D'Artois' office. When we entered, I saw a large Colt Python pistol in a scabbard hanging on a coat rack near a window. D'Artois was one of the lions of power at city hall, but when I shook hands with the tough ex-Marine, he acted as though he was embarrassed that we were there.

He was a hulk of a man, six-feet tall and 260 pounds, with light brown hair and a crew cut and was wearing an expensive suit. I thought he looked like television comedian George Gobel although he outweighed him by one hundred pounds. He had piercing blue-gray eyes that held people in a trance and a constant sad expression on his face. When he spoke, people listened as though he were the representative for some political deity they knew existed but did not understand.

We talked for about five minutes, and as Wilson and I were leaving his office, I heard an inner voice that said, "This man is a crook." I wondered why I would think such a thing. I had never met the man before and, in fact, had never heard his name. The experience in his office that afternoon was quite mystical for I had never had a thought like that before. However, that inner voice was unmistakable and proved to be prophetic.

I did not realize it at the time, but it would soon come to light that he represented the evil side of law enforcement in Shreveport with all its dark secrets.

During the months after my first meeting with the commissioner, I interviewed him a dozen times on various police-related matters. One night, I confronted him about a rumor I had heard from two police officers concerning several young people from well-known Shreveport families who were making fake driver's licenses. They were charging their underage friends, or those who had lost their licenses to DWIs, two hundred dollars for each license. The officers told me the young men had a friend in the photo lab at Barksdale Air Force Base in Bossier City who was helping them and doing the detail work. They all were making a lot of money selling the licenses. When I informed the commissioner of the rumor, he looked surprised. I knew his officers had also told him about the fake driver's license operation, and he had done nothing about it. He immediately picked up the phone and called Lt. Robert Merolla of the Organized Crime and Intelligence Division.

"Robert, do you know anything about kids making up false driver's licenses for some of their friends around town?" the commissioner asked. "I didn't think so."

He hung up the phone and said, "Merolla doesn't know anything about it."

Suddenly I had a very intriguing yet somewhat devious idea.

Garbage collectors had been on strike for several weeks, and tons of stinking garbage was piling up all over the city. Some time later, the city commissioners retained the Southern Research Company to do a study of the causes of the strike and report back to them. However, when the commissioners received the report, they kept it confidential. Some portions indicated the city might have precipitated the strike because of the way the garbage men were treated.

There were many rumors spreading around Shreveport concerning the strike and who may or may not have been culpable. Every reporter in town was trying to get a copy of the Southern Research report.

That evening in D'Artois' office, as we discussed the young people in the fake driver's license scheme, I said, "Commissioner, I don't really want to write a story about these kids, but I sure would like to have a copy of the Southern Research report."

He shoved the report across his desk toward me and responded, "Just don't tell anyone where you got it."

"You have my word," I told him, and I never mentioned to anyone, including McDaniel, how I got my hands on the report.

The next morning the Southern Research report, with certain unfavorable information about city officials, was the top story in our newspaper. I kept my word and never wrote the story about the counterfeit licenses. Captain Burns later told me he had also informed D'Artois about the driver's license scam—and he had named names.[8]

"All he said was, 'When I was seventeen I was a Marine fighting the Japs on Bougainville,'" Burns said the commissioner told him.[9]

On the Monday after the first enterprise team story, McDaniel asked me to come into his office.

"Bill Keith, it will be your responsibility as the city government reporter to follow-up on the articles by the enterprise team."

He never called me "Bill" or "Keith" but always "Bill Keith."

"Yeah, Mr. Mac, I'm okay with that," I replied.

"You're our man at city hall and over there every day. You may take some heat," he said.

"I can handle it," I told him.

The commissioner called a news conference for 10:00 A.M. Monday for the purpose of damage control. He knew that the hard-hitting story had questioned his credibility, and he had to do something to counteract the article and address his alleged wrongdoing. I believe he was so arrogant and intoxicated with power that he thought he could successfully answer all the questions raised by the enterprise team's article in Sunday's paper and dispel any doubts about his leadership of the police department. Moreover, he would count on all the other news media to help him.

When I walked into his office that morning, it was filled with reporters from the afternoon *Journal,* several radio stations, and the three local network television stations. All of them looked at me with suspicion, which was an indication they were either jealous of the enterprise team's scoop or they simply did not believe the story was true. They were anxious to hear what he had to say in answer to our story, and he knew he had a captive audience.

During the early days of our investigation, most of the other reporters in Shreveport considered the commissioner sacrosanct and beyond reproach. They simply could not believe that he could be responsible for any wrongdoing or malfeasance in office. They thought our probe into his questionable activities was just a headline in search of a story.

Those of us at the *Times,* which was a morning newspaper, played a game of cat and mouse with the afternoon *Journal.* We would write an exposé for the morning paper, and the commissioner would respond and defend himself and his actions in the afternoon paper. At one time, I felt the reporters at the *Journal* wanted to give the commissioner a free ride. It often appeared as if they were trying to defend him. I later learned that was not true.

Carl Liberto, the managing editor of the *Journal,* told me in an interview in March of 2006, "At first we thought the story was a lot of brouhaha and that there was nothing to it."

However, beginning with Wray Post of KSLA-TV, the CBS affiliate in our city, the various reporters began to understand the serious nature of our investigation of the commissioner and at that point contributed to uncovering wrongdoing in the police department. I have always appreciated Post and Don Owen, the KSLA news director, for they were well-respected newsmen in our city and their pursuit of the truth added to our own credibility.

At the conference, the commissioner had a solemn look on his face, and as he addressed the room full of reporters, he managed to avoid eye contact with me. During his opening statement, he strongly defended his method of accounting for funds paid to police informants, stating he planned to make all records of the payments available to the city's auditors and to Finance Commissioner Burton.[10] He made it quite clear that regardless of the innuendos in the *Times'* story, the public would have to take his word on how the funds were disbursed.

Guilt is a ghost that haunts its own house, and the commissioner had guilt written all over his face that morning. The only time he ever looked at me was when he flatly denied that he had misappropriated any of the money.

"I've been in this game too long, twenty-five years in the sheriff's office and then in police," he said. "There's no way I've pocketed a dime. This late in the game, I'm not going to change. My integrity is on the line."[11]

Throughout the news conference, the commissioner acted as though he was surprised that anyone would question his actions as the city's top law enforcement officer. He seemed to have a toxic absorption with himself and a total aversion to any kind of accountability. It was clear that his strategy was to feed ideals to the public and lies to the news media. He was a master at manipulation.

When the news conference ended, the reporters rushed out of his office to file their stories. I called McDaniel to give him a summary, then decided to ask Commissioner Burton a few questions. Walking into Burton's office, I noticed his face was drawn and pinched. He told me he thought our newspaper had blown the D'Artois informant story way out of proportion.

"If he [D'Artois] says he can account for the funds he can account for them," Burton said.[12]

Burton was a no-nonsense, straightforward public servant. There was never any hint of scandal or impropriety in his office. He was simply following protocol in defending D'Artois, a fellow member of the city council.

I spent the rest of the day at city hall checking on several other stories for the paper and discovered that most everyone was talking about the allegations in the Sunday *Times*. I also detected that two members of the commissioner's personal public relations staff were following me, and that gave me the creeps. He apparently wanted to know the names of everyone I had interviewed that afternoon, particularly the police officers. Subsequently, he called some of them into his office to grill them about the nature of our talk.

There was a lot of tension in the halls of the police department. While covering my beat, I had befriended several police officers, but that afternoon, none of them would speak to or even look at me. When I met them in the halls, they just turned away as though I didn't exist. That day I felt like a wooden horse on a carousel gliding up and down but going nowhere.

Finally, Kenneth Lanigan, chief of detectives, broke the silence. I asked him if I could use his telephone to call my city editor at the newspaper, and he said yes. One of the commissioner's PR men, Chuck Carter, who was a former police reporter for the newspaper, followed me to Lanigan's office and eavesdropped on my telephone conversation. He also listened in on my discussion with Lanigan. I presume he then reported to the commissioner what he had heard.

Lanigan was a tough Irish cop whose police exploits had been the subject of articles in national magazines. He was a legend in the department, having arrested some of the worst criminals in the Shreveport-Bossier City area. He had also been involved in a highly publicized shootout with an armed robber who shot him several times before Lanigan, the only cop on the scene, finally killed him. When Lanigan's captain arrived on the scene and saw that Lanigan had multiple gunshot wounds, he turned around and just drove away, leaving him to die.

"I never understood why my captain did that," Lanigan told me.

Fortunately, another officer drove by and took him to the hospital where the doctors said he had barely enough blood to keep him alive. Some thought Lanigan was cynical, but he had seen shootings, stabbings, drowning, and poisonings. Crime had littered the city streets like a toilet that run over and wouldn't flush. But cynical? I don't think so. Maybe just sick of it all. I didn't have to be Ironside to figure that out.

Two other police officers, Lt. Robert Merolla, who worked for Captain Burns in the Organized Crime and Intelligence Division, and Maj. Jim Byrd, head of the Division of Special Investigations, helped me during our investigation. The commissioner called these two men and Kelley, Burns, and Lanigan, the "Dirty Five." In time, it became apparent that they had made up their minds to try to clean up the department even if it meant they had to risk their lives.

I like to remember these men as Shreveport's version of the "Untouchables." They, along with my editor and the enterprise team, provided a service to the public that in the early days of the investigation was not understood or appreciated.

Lanigan, Chief Kelley, and Captain Burns became my good friends. When I needed help with a story, I could call them at any hour. Although they would never give me exact information, they told me where to look for the skeletons that were buried throughout the police department and kept me informed on just about everything the commissioner was doing.

The enterprise team had taken the first step in seeking some accountability from the commissioner. But as future stories unfolded and dramatic events occurred, we all realized that the newspaper had opened Pandora's Box.

After the first story appeared, there was no indication that the people of Shreveport were even remotely concerned. They didn't seem to care about what the commissioner was up to. Even Mayor Calhoun Allen's response to the revelations about Commissioner D'Artois in our newspaper was as predictable as sin following temptation. When Marsha Shuler, another *Times* reporter, and I interviewed him for a response to our story, he became livid with anger as he lashed out at the *Times* in general and me in particular for raising questions about how the commissioner handled the funds.[13]

"We are not going to be destroyed by the *Shreveport Times* or any other news media," the mayor told us during the interview.

"Mayor, our newspaper is not trying to destroy anyone," I told him. "We're trying to find the truth about Mr. D'Artois' payments to police informants."

Shreveport mayor Calhoun Allen defended D'Artois during a press conference and predicted the commissioner would be cleared of all charges. (Courtesy LSUS Archives—Noel Memorial Library)

His hands were shaking, his voice quivering, and his face lost all its color as he answered our questions. Later, I wondered if he had cards he wasn't showing or if he was stressed out because he had learned that the enterprise team was carefully examining his travel records, particularly money he had received for charter flights for which there were no receipts.

Then he added the article's revelation in no way reflected on city hall. To me that was his twisted equivalent of saying, "I'm okay, city hall's okay, but there's something wrong with you guys at the newspaper." I wondered if he had been reading the newspaper upside down.

Allen also issued a warning, saying, "We will fight back," if the *Times* doesn't back off the city hall investigation. However, he did not elaborate on any action he might take.[14]

"I'm not going to allow any commissioner to be destroyed by you or anyone else," he told us.

"Mr. Mayor, the *Shreveport Times* has no desire to destroy anyone," I replied.

The mayor said he found "nothing unusual or strange" about D'Artois' accounting method. "Nothing unusual—absolutely nothing. You talk to any city in the country and they do the same thing."

What he said was making no sense at all to me. I realized that he and the other lions of power at city hall had been on a free ride with zero responsibility for their actions. Apparently he didn't like the "handwriting on the wall" that said he and the other commissioners were going to have to make some changes.

He said that in spite of the investigation, "I think everyone [at city hall] is interested in doing things to benefit the people of this city."

I had always believed that Mayor Allen was a rather decent fellow but depended too much on Commissioner D'Artois to tell him how to run the affairs of the city. The mayor's nephew, attorney James Thornton, once told me, "Uncle Calhoun is a good dancer, and he knows how to hold a chair for a lady to get seated in a nice restaurant, but D'Artois calls all the shots at city hall."

Chief Kelley and Captain Burns had informed McDaniel that the commissioner and perhaps some other city officials, including the mayor, were using city funds for personal charter flights for leisure and recreational purposes. McDaniel decided that this lead would be the enterprise team's next major story.

A careful survey of charter travel expenditures revealed that there were no itemized records concerning destination or purpose of the travel for either the mayor or the commissioner. Both men often withdrew large sums of money for travel but did not account for disbursement of the funds.[15]

Concerning the mayor's travel, the team reported, "Many of his trips have not been documented with records justifying expenditures or reflecting return of unspent money." They also pointed out that the commissioner often traveled by charter plane and rarely gave any reason for the trip or the destination. Team members documented numerous charter flights to Hot Springs, Arkansas, home of the Oaklawn Park Racetrack.

There was sufficient evidence to corroborate the commissioner's addictive gambling habits both at Oaklawn and at Louisiana Downs in Bossier City. Stanley Tiner, the former editor of the afternoon *Shreveport Journal,* once told me that his newspaper had a "deep throat" in the police department who had informed him of D'Artois' gambling problem and how he might be paying for it.

Tiner, who now is the editor of the *Sun Herald* in Biloxi, Mississippi, has received national awards for journalistic excellence, including a Pulitzer Prize in 2006 for coverage of Hurricane Katrina. When he heard the rumors about the commissioner, he assigned reporter Alan Stonecipher and photographer Lawrence Lea to follow D'Artois and document his gambling habit at the local racetrack, particularly during working hours when he was supposed to be at his office.

When the *Journal* investigation was complete, Stonecipher went to D'Artois, confronted him with the information he had on his gambling, and asked him if he wanted to respond to the story. Furious, the commissioner refused to answer any of Stonecipher's questions. Rather, he called Douglas Attaway, the owner and publisher of the newspaper, and asked to meet with him and Tiner.

"He was very upset that we were writing a story about his gambling and urged us not to run it," Tiner said. "So, Mr. Attaway killed the story."

Tiner, who had served as a *Times* reporter and editorial writer before he was named editor of the *Journal,* was one of the best newsmen in the history of the two Shreveport newspapers. He was a gifted writer and a courageous investigator and was disappointed when Attaway told him the newspaper would not carry the story. He considered it a dark day for journalism in Shreveport.

Even though he decided not to tell the public about D'Artois' gambling, Attaway had many good qualities and was greatly admired by the people of Shreveport. He was a strong advocate of law and order and the idea of going after D'Artois, who more than anyone else in Northwest Louisiana represented that law and order, was unthinkable.

However, there were other reasons.

"George controlled the rioting back in the sixties, established law and order, and built up a first-rate police department, and Mr. Attaway didn't want to rock the boat," Carl Liberto, the managing editor of the *Journal,* told me.[16]

He said that before Tiner became the *Journal*'s editor, George Shannon, a strong segregationist, was the editor. According to Liberto, who grew up in Shreveport, D'Artois was a part of the pervasive, gambling culture in the city so it was only natural for him to spend a lot of time at the racetrack. In addition, he said he had observed gambling in the back rooms of several of the downtown bars and night clubs, yet the commissioner made no effort to try to stop it.

"George was getting a cut from all the bars downtown, and when they decided to quit paying him, he busted them," Liberto said.

Liberto believed there were a number of people, particularly in the Italian community, who believed that gambling was connected to the New Orleans mob. He even "saw several of [Carlos] Marcello's men in the Kon Tiki Restaurant in Shreveport," saying, "I knew who they were and where they were from."

Carlos Marcello was the *Mafia* chieftain who controlled the New Orleans underworld for nearly fifty years.

I also later learned that a local television affiliate in Shreveport had been investigating D'Artois' gambling but for some undisclosed reason decided not to carry the report. I have wondered if D'Artois was able to convince someone in authority at the station to kill the story.

That was the mindset of the various news media in Shreveport. Hence, politicians could lie, cheat, and steal, and yet the people who depended on the news media to keep them informed on such matters never learned of the wrongdoing by the city leaders.

Meanwhile, on Wednesday, May 5, Finance Commissioner Burton had concluded that the *Times* story was not going to go away. As a result, he authorized the Southern Research Company of Shreveport, an organization with a number of top-flight investigators, to look into D'Artois' payments to informants.

"I told Southern Research to examine the payments made out of the investigative funds and to do whatever other investigative work they wish to do in connection with the funds," Burton told the *Journal*. "I want them to see if these funds are being handled as we have naturally assumed they are being handled—in accordance with normal police practices."[17]

About that time, Jim Montgomery, in a *Times* editorial, called on Mayor Allen and the city council to conduct a thorough audit of certain critical areas identified in reports by the newspaper's enterprise team.

"It is necessary to concentrate on first things first," Montgomery said.

> These areas, specifically, are:
> The slipshod accounting by Public Safety Commissioner George D'Artois of city funds issued to him personally for the stated purpose of paying informants in criminal investigations.

The sketchy expense report procedures used by Mr. D'Artois and Mayor Allen in their accounting of city funds used for travel expenses and in the extensive use of chartered airplanes.

Montgomery added, "These areas have already been pinpointed by *Times* reporters, and so far city hall has not come up with full, satisfactory answers to questions raised by the reports."

He went on to point out that all of Commissioner D'Artois' subordinates are required to keep meticulous records of their expenditures to police informants.

"Why, then, should Mr. D'Artois not have to account to someone for money issued to him personally for this purpose?" Montgomery asked. "As for the travel expense reports, these date back at least three and four years, with no explanation of what the money was spent for, what the purpose of the trip was, or even the destinations of some of the trips, many of them made on chartered airplanes. We feel that the citizens of Shreveport deserve some far better answers to the questions that have been raised. There are specific critical areas that should be investigated now."[18]

The Shreveport Police Department where D'Artois served as the most powerful lawman in Louisiana.

CHAPTER SIX

D'Artois, the Lawman

Since the turn of the twentieth century, Louisiana has been a breeding ground for every kind of political corruption known to man. Most of it began in the late 1920s with the bedeviled leadership of former governor Huey Pierce Long. Although he did not invent political scandal, it flourished under his administration.

In order for us to understand Commissioner D'Artois, we must understand the corrupt legacy of Governor Long. A number of politicians in Louisiana, including D'Artois at least to a degree, followed Long's examples. They believed that as elected officials, they had a right to steal from the public, and sadly, his twisted legacy permeates and defines politics in Louisiana to this day.

Driving east out of Dallas for about three hours on Interstate 20, a superhighway cut through the Piney Woods of East Texas and rolling ranch land with endless fields of dancing wildflowers, bluebonnets, and Indian paintbrush, you enter Louisiana. On the border between the two states, a welcome sign greets you in both French and English: *"Bienvenue en Louisiane,* Welcome to Louisiana."

You then pass the American Rose Center, the Fair Grounds, and Independence Stadium, home of the Independence Bowl. Next, you will see the jagged Shreveport skyline and are just a few minutes away from downtown Shreveport on the banks of the Red River. Take a left on Spring Street to Texas Street and you will see the majestic First United Methodist Church at the head of Texas Street, looking down on Shreveport like a guardian angel. That road runs into Murphy Street and to the Shreveport Police Department offices at city hall where George D'Artois once ruled like a feudal lord over the largest police department in North Louisiana as the most powerful lawman in the state.

79

Ironically, almost in the shadow of city hall, where the wealthy and elite regularly received preferential treatment from the city's bureaucrats, there were rows of shotgun houses, drug dens, and sleazy night spots heavy with the smell of marijuana into which the patrons carried Saturday-night specials, knives, and straight razors. The neighborhood was seedy, with run-down storefronts, sign-cluttered eyesores, and piles of trash and garbage littering the streets, a classic example of the way a city shouldn't look. Poor and unemployed black men stood on the street corners drinking beer, enduring the awful summer heat and hopelessly watching Shreveport and the world pass them by.

Prostitutes walked the streets at night looking for johns to take to a run-down motel to turn a trick to get money. They also carried straight razors strapped to their legs and would cut your throat in a minute. Some called them "straight-razor-totin' women, some real bad mamas."

It was never big news in Shreveport, a city with a deep cultural chasm between whites and blacks, when a black man got his throat cut in a nightclub in the Bottoms or Allendale or was killed during a gambling game. Shreveport citizens grew accustomed to it for it happened every Saturday night. The white establishment elite looked on these killings as just one less black person to cause trouble in the city. The *Shreveport Times* seldom gave coverage to these killings in our daily police reports. We knew it just didn't matter to the white people in the city who read our newspaper.

This was the Shreveport of George D'Artois. D'Artois was born on Christmas Day in 1925, the son of William F. and Mary Holmes D'Artois, both natives of Shreveport. He graduated from high school in the city and attended Centenary College of Louisiana in Shreveport and Louisiana State University in Baton Rouge, where he studied business administration.

During World War II, he served in the United States Marine Corps. D'Artois was only seventeen years old when he went ashore on the island of Bougainville in the South Pacific and fought and defeated the Japanese defenders. He also fought in several other battles during the war, and by the time he was eighteen, he had already become a combat-hardened jungle fighter. At age twenty, his commander promoted him to sergeant. He served in the Marine Corps for three years and, when the war ended, was honorably discharged.

He married the former Billie Claire Best, a beautiful woman with dark eyes and careless hair, and together, they had three children: a son, George Wendell, Jr., and two daughters, Mary Cecile and Elaine Claire.

D'Artois joined the Caddo Parish Sheriff's Office in 1952 where he served with distinction as a deputy. His political journey began in 1961 when he resigned from the sheriff's office, after serving for nine years, to seek the office of commissioner of public safety in the City of Shreveport. The voters elected him commissioner the following year. He soundly defeated the incumbent, J. Earl Downs, and it became apparent that he was popular with the voters. He was reelected in 1966, 1970, and 1974.

As commissioner of public safety, D'Artois was the city's top law enforcement officer and also supervisor of the fire department. Well known throughout America as an innovative law enforcement officer, he served as a lecturer at the Louisiana State University Law Enforcement Institute in Baton Rouge and at the Southwestern Legal Foundation at Southern Methodist University in Dallas for several years.

In 1973, the National Police Officers Association of America recognized him for his contribution to law enforcement. D'Artois also received praise in an editorial appearing in the *Shreveport Journal.*

It should be remembered that four times the voters of Shreveport elected George D'Artois to public office. Four times they had faith enough to entrust him with the management of their public safety department.

In return, he gave the city improvements in the department's services and helped build facilities that were badly needed.[1]

D'Artois was a popular lawman among whites in the city; a city with a number of White Citizens' Council members. They opposed the 1954 United States Supreme Court ruling that abolished school segregation in the *Brown v. Board of Education of Topeka* decision. Thousands of white segregationists in Louisiana joined the councils through which they could voice their opposition to integration.

There was also some Ku Klux Klan activity in the Shreveport area during his first and second terms as commissioner. Hundreds of Klan members held rallies in the area, including one in Mooringsport, a few miles north of Shreveport. A large number of Klan members reportedly lived in the town of Blanchard, a suburb of Shreveport. Even today, some blacks are reluctant to drive through the town.

As one black man said, "The Klan down there in Blanchard is heavy; they down there waiting for you."

The black community of Shreveport had a love-hate relationship with D'Artois. He allowed bars and nightclubs in black neighborhoods to stay open after closing hours, enabling them to make a lot of extra money. They paid the commissioner well for that privilege and the protection he provided for them from his own police officers.

One black gambler told me that at times when D'Artois and his men broke up the gambling games, things could get ugly. The gambler said the commissioner threatened his life one night when he and several of his police officers raided a high-stakes gambling game in Shreveport:

"There were a number of high rollers in the game with thousands of dollars in each pot. D'Artois and his men came busting in, and he put a revolver up against my temple and said 'out-of-town gamblers aren't welcome in Shreveport' and if he ever saw me again, he would blow my brains out."

Then he said D'Artois took the money off the table, and he and his officers returned to their patrol cars. A police report was never filed on the action at the gambling house that night.

Through the months and years, I became acquainted with dozens of police officers and most of them were men of integrity who had a great passion for police work. At times, in private, they told me stories of how white officers would beat up black prisoners while handcuffed in the police department elevator going from the booking desk, in the basement, to the second-floor jail. When the elevator door slammed shut, the officers brutalized the prisoners with nightsticks, often leaving them bruised and bloodied. The code of silence among the officers kept the true reasoning for the beatings hidden. The official causes were filed as "resisting arrest."

However, when Kelley became chief of police, he made it quite clear that he was a strong advocate of law and order for everyone, including his officers. It didn't take him long to prove that he was a man of his word and wouldn't put up with the elevator beatings. When two white police officers killed a black man on the Texas Street Bridge, Kelley arrested them, and they were tried, convicted, and sent to prison.[2]

Later Melvin Collins, Sr., the editor of the *Shreveport Sun,* a black-owned weekly newspaper with a strong voice for racial equality, wrote an editorial, saying, "There is a new day in law enforcement in Shreveport when a white man is convicted of killing a black man."

However, D'Artois consistently repressed demonstrations in the black community, and that created fear in the hearts of the blacks but admiration and respect from the whites in the city.

As he gained power, D'Artois became a master of deceit.

On June 21, 1975, I attended a meeting of the Downtown Rotary Club in the old historic Captain Shreve Hotel. D'Artois was the featured speaker. During his speech, he informed the Rotarians, some of the most influential men in the city, that he had formed a special police unit to monitor violence-prone Shreveport nightclubs, particularly in the black community. D'Artois knew exactly how to pander to a white crowd. He said that the special squad had recently raided several nightclubs, finding ten concealed handguns and making several arrests:

This is a selected police division, which includes both undercover and uniformed policemen, and we believe it will cut down on the killings in these clubs.

The problem we face is that seventy-five to eighty percent of the people we arrest will receive suspended sentences or pardons and will be back on the streets. We seem to be trying to make Holiday Inns out of our prisons. We try to rehabilitate the criminals in a week so they can get back on the streets of Shreveport. People who have committed crimes of violence shouldn't be back on the street where they are able to commit crimes again. It's time we began thinking about the victims rather than the criminals.

After receiving a hearty applause, he told the story of the arrest of a Shreveport man who had raped a fifteen-year-old girl. The man was convicted of the crime but received only a one-year prison sentence in Angola, the Louisiana State Penitentiary. The rapist served six months and was released and returned to Shreveport.

"After he returned, he raped a seven-year-old child," D'Artois said.

It was apparent to me that day that D'Artois knew all the right things to say to an ultra-conservative group of Shreveport businessmen. He distracted their attention away from any rumors of graft and corruption they had heard or misgivings they harbored about him.

D'Artois was also a champion of both daily newspapers in the city. For a number of years, the papers failed to hold him accountable for not shutting down the hundreds of illegal payoff pinball machines in the city. The newspapers had received numerous complaints from some of the gamblers' wives who said their husbands had lost all their money on the machines, and they were not able to pay their rent, car notes, or buy groceries for the children. However, the newspapers didn't even look into the problem.

In the May 19, 1974, editions, a *Shreveport Times* editorial writer praised D'Artois for the good job he was doing for the people of the city. The writer pointed out that a new highly advanced computerized traffic system, whereby all traffic lights in the city would be synchronized to help the flow of traffic, would be installed by the end of 1974 and would facilitate traffic on the busy city streets.

> In many respects the first-in-the-nation status of this communications system is representative of the top-rate Police Department that has grown up in the city during the past dozen years. It is the planning-ahead attitude of department leaders that has brought about such excellence.
>
> The common thread that cannot be ignored in all these gains is the leadership of Public Safety Commissioner George D'Artois. During his 12 years as commissioner, Mr. D'Artois has built a Public Safety Department of which all Shreveporters can be proud.

Concerning the synchronized traffic light system in the city, the newspaper would have done well to have followed the progress of that system more closely. During the 1968 bond issue, the people of Shreveport voted several hundred thousand dollars for the innovative new system, but it was never installed.

One day, years later, McNutt asked me to look into what became of the money. I interviewed D'Artois, Mayor Allen, and Finance Commissioner Burton, but no one could tell me anything about the money. "Could it just have disappeared into thin air?" I asked. No one seemed to know, and it was evident they didn't want to talk about it. Furthermore, no one seemed to care.

Mayor Allen said the money probably was used for other worthwhile causes. Of course, that presented a dilemma for the public officials since citizens who voted for the bond issue designated the money for the traffic system, not for some other worthwhile project.

Since the funds were earmarked for D'Artois' department, he would have been the only one who knew for sure what happened to the money; however, his reply was "I just don't know what happened to that money." The city never installed the system, and no one ever learned how the money was spent.

The *Times* editorial writer also pointed out that there had been several years of social and racial upheaval throughout the United States, but "Shreveport has been spared" and that D'Artois should receive the credit.

City leaders liked to boast that there was no racial segregation in Shreveport. Throughout D'Artois' reign, all members of the city council were elected from at-large rather than single-member districts, and as a result, the large black population had no influence whatsoever in city government since none could get elected to public office.

United States district judge Benjamin Dawkins, Jr. of Shreveport struck down the enabling ordinance for the at-large districts and, for the first time in history, opened the door for blacks to participate in local government. Occasionally white officials would appoint "a token nigger" to some board so they could boast that there was no segregation in the city. However, prior to 1976, Shreveport was one of the most segregated cities in the South.

What the *Times* editorial writer failed to mention was that D'Artois kept down racial violence through intimidation. For instance, on Sunday, September 22, 1963, the threat of a confrontation between blacks and police hung heavily over the city.[3] One week before, four young black girls were killed when a bomb exploded at the Sixteenth Street Baptist Church in Birmingham, Alabama.

Pres. John F. Kennedy proclaimed September 22 a day of national mourning, and the national office of the National Association for the Advancement of Colored People (NAACP) asked all the local chapters to hold memorial services on that day.

A group of blacks in Shreveport asked Commissioner D'Artois for a permit to march from the District Auditorium on Kenneth Avenue and Milam Street to Little Union Baptist Church at 1846 Milam, only a few blocks away.[4] The black leaders also announced that there would be a religious service at the church after the march.

The Reverend Harry Blake, a young Baptist preacher and civil rights activist, was one of the three ministers who signed the permit request for the march. The black Baptist Ministers Alliance, the United Christian Movement, and the NAACP sponsored the Birmingham Memorial March.

D'Artois knew a lot more about the plans for the march than the organizers realized. He had secretly placed an illegal listening device in the NAACP offices, which recorded the proceedings of all their meetings. Then he would transcribe the proceedings, print hundreds of copies, and distribute them to various influential white leaders in the community. Both daily newspapers received copies of the transcripts. Although it was patently illegal, there is no record of anyone ever speaking out against the secret recordings.

In a curt letter, D'Artois denied the request for the march. He informed the organizers of the march that the police department would maintain law and order "regardless of a few individuals and organizations who want to destroy our American way of life."[5] The commissioner not only denied the permit for the march, he also warned the black community that he would take stern measures against anyone who defied his order. He was well aware that his strong law-and-order rhetoric would play well among the white majority in the city.

Exactly what happened that Sunday afternoon in September is still hidden in a cloak of mystery. Both newspapers reported that a march provoked a confrontation with police; others say no march ever occurred. Nonetheless, there was a violent racial incident that afternoon.

"Reverberations were felt for days, even years, afterwards," wrote Craig Flournoy years later in the *Journal*. "And the old claim among whites that Shreveport had 'good race relations' was effectively destroyed."[6]

About 4:15 P.M., city trucks carrying armed police officers began arriving in the Milam Street area. They were equipped with riot guns, shotguns, submachine guns, automatic rifles, pistols, and tear gas. A short time later, several officers in the mounted patrol unit arrived on horseback along with police cars and motorcycle patrolmen. D'Artois had assembled a formidable army of some two hundred police officers and sheriff's deputies.

When he ordered the riot squads into action, they marched shoulder to shoulder in military precision down the middle of Milam Street toward Little Union Baptist Church, pushing aside anyone who got in their way.

Police officer Rocky Gamel, who was an eyewitness, said there must have been at least a thousand people, most of them just bystanders, on Milam Street that day.[7]

The Reverend Blake said those attending the worship service inside the church felt as if they were under a state of siege.[8] "There were policemen and deputies with bayonets on their rifles and with electric cow prods," Blake explained to me some years later. "I felt like we were being held hostage.[9]

According to Blake, Jesse Stone, who later became president of Southern University in Baton Rouge, went to D'Artois and told him the attendees wanted to leave the church. The commissioner told Stone to send them out two by two. Except for Blake and a few others, most of the people left the church.

"About that time, I heard a commotion outside the church, and when I went to check on it, three policemen and D'Artois met me, and two of the policemen pulled me outside and began beating me," Blake remembered. "I still have the scars . . . every officer who could get a piece of me with his billy club stepped in. When they felt they had enough, or thought that I was dead, they left me lifeless in the [church] driveway."

One of the policemen hit him so hard that his skull was split open. According to one eyewitness, after the merciless beating, the police officers stood around laughing and playing with their billy clubs.

Since Blake was trying to protect his head from the beating, he told me he wasn't sure if D'Artois had taken part. "But he was with the policemen who struck me," he said. "He later denied that he ever hit me."

Blake explained to me that some of the events of the day had been greatly embellished by the news media, including the story that officer Bill Beckett rode his horse inside the church and started beating the people with his nightstick.

"That never happened," Reverend Blake said. "But the officers did ride their horses across the vestibule in front of the church."

After the beating, Blake's friends called an ambulance, which took him to a hospital in Dallas.

"They were taking me to Dallas. Because I was beaten by the police here; how safe would I be with doctors here?" Blake asked, recalling that September 23 morning so many years ago.

"Forty years have passed, the injuries have healed, and yet the Rev. Blake sees the scars are still there—open wounds on the history of Shreveport," wrote Don Walker of the *Times* years later.[10]

Today, the Reverend Blake is one of the most distinguished ministers in America. He is the pastor of Mt. Canaan Baptist Church in Shreveport, a church with a proud history, and serves as president of the Louisiana Baptist Convention and general secretary of the National Baptist Convention, USA, Inc., the nation's oldest and largest African American religious organization with some 7.5 million members.

CHAPTER SEVEN

The Missing Records

Once the enterprise team's initial stories about Commissioner D'Artois were printed, the *Shreveport Times* became an unpopular newspaper with many of our readers who could not believe what they were reading about the commissioner.

Every day I went to city hall to cover my beat. During the early days of our investigation of the commissioner, certain police officers were trying to work their way through the shock of the revelations of the commissioner's wrongdoing; others were in denial.

But some of our readers believed in what we were doing and supported us. We learned that the B-52 pilots and crews at Barksdale Air Force Base, in Bossier City, who were "on the pad," i.e. twenty-four hour alert in case of a nuclear crisis, sent out for the *Times* each morning. They read the stories and discussed the investigation in their alert headquarters. In addition, a journalism class at Texas Christian University, in Fort Worth, several hours away from Shreveport, studied the *Times* in an investigative reporting class. The journalism classes at Centenary College and LSU-Shreveport also read and discussed our stories each day.

Those of us in the newsroom were so caught up in the drama of the investigation of the commissioner that we were not aware of the impact the dramatic events unfolding at city hall were having throughout the region and state.

During our investigation, I learned that through the years D'Artois had practiced selective law enforcement in the city. For instance, if a young man from a wealthy family were to get into some kind of trouble with the police, D'Artois often handled the case himself. He would call the parents and inform them that their son or daughter had been arrested for driving without a valid driver's license or under the influence of alcohol or perhaps with a stash of marijuana.

Then D'Artois would say something like, "But I know he is a good boy and I'm going to bring him home, and you should encourage him to stay out of trouble." He would also promise the parents that he would see to it that there would be no record of the son or daughter's arrest.

However, if a young man or woman from "across the tracks" or from the black community was arrested for the same offense, they would have to go to jail and appear in court. In these cases, there would be a permanent record of the offense in the police department.

We documented cases where D'Artois ordered the police department's central records division to destroy the arrest records, including fingerprints and mug shots, of three young men. Two of them were the sons of D'Artois' friends.

"I was asked to pull the fingerprint cards by the young boys, and I did it because of their age," D'Artois told the *Journal* after our newspaper exposed the practice. "I would have done it for any young person for a minor offense."[1]

Chief Kelley and Asst. Chief Walter Cash took signed statements from certain employees of the identification division who said D'Artois ordered them to alter the records of the three young men. Under Louisiana law, the alteration of police documents is punishable by a year in jail and a one-thousand-dollar fine.

Although the commissioner did not keep records of his payments to confidential informants, he kept meticulous records of all the young men and women he helped and the names, addresses, and telephone numbers of their parents. He knew they would be prospective donors to his next reelection campaign.

On May 7, as I made the rounds of the various offices at city hall looking for stories for the next day's editions of the newspaper, I decided to go to the booking desk in the basement of the police

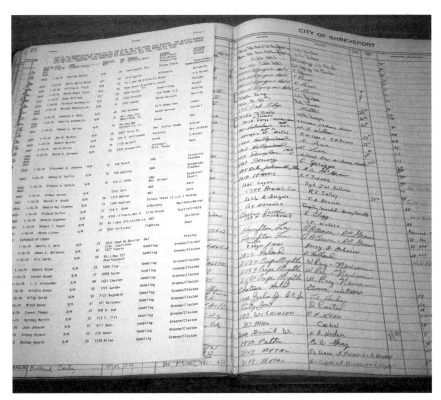

The infamous police patrol booking desk book. The author discovered that names of certain criminals had been removed from the book and destroyed to keep them from going to trial.

department to look through the Record of Arrest Book. It was right after roll call for the evening shift and the place was in a happy state of hysterics. Police officers were coming and going, bringing in perpetrators in handcuffs and in a hurry to get back out on the streets.

Maj. Charlie Justice, the watch commander, was nervous, as if he had just seen an epiphany, and Commissioner D'Artois, being interviewed by the other newspaper, said that the *Times* reporters were running around city hall like a pack of rats.

The booking desk was not my favorite place for there were times when the men being arrested smelled of alcohol and soiled underwear. Some of the drunks unzipped their pants and tried to urinate on the officers—right there in front of the booking desk. Others were high enough for a moonwalk.

Police Sgt. Ernie Gullion was in charge of the desk that afternoon. Two other officers assisted him. Their job was to "book" each suspect arrested by a patrolman or detective in the Record of Arrest Book and send them on to the city jail to await arraignment or bail.

McDaniel, after his meeting with Chief Kelley and Captain Burns, told me that gamblers were receiving preferential treatment and protection from D'Artois but that Captain Burns' detectives were making some arrests. Lanigan confirmed this and suggested I look into the gambling arrests.

"I'm getting a little tired of my detectives 'busting' gambling games, putting their lives on the line, only to have the paperwork disappear and none of the gamblers ever going to trial," Lanigan told me.

Much to my surprise, I discovered that in January of that year seventeen gamblers had been arrested, booked, and ordered to appear in court. I noticed Sergeant Gullion seemed a little nervous when I began examining the books, but we both knew they were public records.

Gullion, who was close to D'Artois, apparently told him that I had been looking at the gambling arrests. The commissioner knew that if I probed deep enough I would uncover a secret that would be a public embarrassment to both him and the department.

Although D'Artois had been providing protection for the gamblers and was well paid for doing so, Chief Kelley and Captain Burns had found a way to break up the games, and there wasn't anything the commissioner could do about it. Kelley would order Burns to break up the games, and when D'Artois complained, Burns would respond by saying he was following the chief's orders.

This arrangement posed a dilemma for the commissioner so he came up with a creative yet devious plan to keep the gamblers from going to court. It worked like this: when the police officers arrested the gamblers—and confiscated all the money on the table—D'Artois ordered the desk sergeant or other booking-desk officers to give him all the arrest records rather than sending them on to the city courts. Then he placed the records in a special file in his office.

Therefore, even though the gamblers were arrested, they were never summoned to appear in court or held accountable for breaking the law. Then, someone in the police department would steal the money confiscated in the gambling raids from the envelopes in the evidence room. No one knows for sure what became of that money. Several officers may have been involved in the charade.

The commissioner thought it was an ingenious plan, and it had worked for years until I started searching through the books. Then it would be a simple matter for me to compare the arrests with the court dockets to see if the gamblers had appeared before a judge.

Sergeant Gullion watched me write down the names of seventeen gamblers, the addresses where they were arrested, and the dates. When he reported what I had done, the commissioner ordered him to destroy all the pages in the Record of Arrest Book that recorded the arrests. (Gullion confessed to me several months later that he was the one who cut out the pages from the book, which was a felony offense, saying he had no idea of the seriousness of the matter and that he was just following orders from the commissioner.)

The next day when I discovered several pages were missing from the book, I immediately informed Chief Kelley who reported the missing records to the commissioner.

The commissioner, in a grandstand play for the news media in the city, ordered Chief Kelley to launch a full-scale investigation into who might have removed the pages from the book. That order was the epitome of hypocrisy on his part. He and I both knew who had ordered the pages removed.

When I examined the clerk of court's records, I found that there were no tickets received in the clerk's office on the seventeen gamblers and that no charging affidavits had been made.[2] Predictably, the commissioner said that the disclosure of the missing records was only "a new attack" on the part of the newspaper to discredit him and the police department. He did not elaborate on what he meant by "a new attack" against him.

During a news conference the next afternoon, the commissioner repeatedly tried to explain that reporters, bail bondsmen, and others had access to the police record book and could have removed the pages. He further stated that his department kept a back-up system to protect the records in the book.[3]

"We have reproduced copies of the three missing pages and have them available for the news media," he said. "We will furnish the city court with these 17 names along with the other names so that they can get bonds for these people for them to appear in court."[4]

What D'Artois failed to mention that day was that all seventeen of the gamblers had been arrested in January, five months earlier, yet not one of them had appeared in court, in spite of his complete back-up system. The gambling reports were so slow they might as well have been coming in by jungle drums.

I believe the commissioner kept a personal set of records in his files to make sure he received his payoffs for keeping the gamblers out of court.

In my search of the Record of Arrest Book, I found nine more names that Sergeant Gullion had failed to destroy. On May 9, I wrote that twenty-six gamblers had been arrested in Shreveport and then released without prosecution because the records of their arrests were never forwarded on to the clerk of the court.[5]

In another development, that Friday evening I asked the clerk of the court Ed Crump if he would return to city hall, after working hours, to allow me to search the court records for information concerning the twenty-six gamblers. Crump, who was a very dedicated public official, opened up his office and his records to me and helped me in my search through the record books.

While we were there, he received a phone call. I overheard parts of the conversation, and when he hung up the phone, I asked him if it was D'Artois who had called.

"Yes, it was, but I don't know how he knew that I was here after working hours," Crump replied.

D'Artois had spies throughout city hall, reporting my every move. Therefore, it was only logical to believe they also were watching Crump. I asked Crump if D'Artois said anything to him concerning my investigation of the court records.

"D'Artois just told me to tell Keith that a lot of records are lost between the time people are charged by the police department and the time they reach the clerk's office."

"Is that a correct assessment?" I asked.

"No. It's very rare for us not to get the records," he responded. "They usually are in our books in a day or two."

Crump then said that D'Artois asked him not to tell me that he had called and that he wanted to see him in his office after I completed my research. However, Crump, in a signal show of courage, refused to go to the commissioner's office and returned to his home immediately after I finished looking through the records. Neither of us ever learned how D'Artois found out we were in the clerk's office after closing hours that evening for we saw no one in the halls that night.

When I walked out of the building, the temperature was in the hundreds, there was a full moon, and all the crazies were out on the streets; but, besides that, everything seemed to be okay. It was just another day in River City.

Chief Kelley told reporters he thought the important thing was to find out who cut the records out of the book.[6]

"The back-up records are very important but we cannot minimize the fact that a permanent record has been destroyed," he said.

Major Justice, who had supervised the record book since 1970, stated that this was the first time any of the pages had ever disappeared.

After the pages were found to be missing, the commissioner requested that Captain Burns meet him in his office. Burns related the following conversation to me[7]:

"When I got to his office his secretary told me he [the commissioner] wanted to meet me in the commissioner's office in the police garage," Burns said. "I went in to the office there and noticed that he had all the shades drawn."

"You're going to take the responsibility for the pages that are missing," Burns said the commissioner informed him.

"No, Commissioner, I'm not going to do it."

Then Burns said the commissioner gazed at him with a crazed look in his eyes and asked, "How many years do you have on the police force?"

"Sixteen."

"You'll never make twenty."

"That meant one of two things," Burns said. "He could have me fired or have me killed."

One day as I was discussing the missing gambling records with Chief of Detectives Lanigan, he gave me a tip that proved to be devastating to the commissioner. Lanigan said that when his men broke up a gambling game, they routinely confiscated the cards, dice, money, and sometimes weapons. These items were placed in a large manila envelope that was stored in the vault behind the booking desk.

Although the contents of the vault were not public record, Major Justice granted me permission to enter and examine all the envelopes on file. There in the evidence room amid the hundreds of files that recorded the history of law and order and crime and punishment in Shreveport, I felt a sense of awe.

A list of the contents was written on the outside of each envelope. The information generally documented any weapons confiscated during the raid, gambling paraphernalia, money, and time, date, and location of the raid. I searched until I found the envelopes marked with the names of the twenty-six suspects who were arrested but never went to trial. Some of the envelopes were soiled and faded with time, and I could hardly read the information written on them.

I decided to check several of the envelopes and compare the

contents to the data written on the front of the envelope. When I opened the first envelope, I was shocked. The arresting officer had noted that several hundred dollars had been confiscated when he broke up the game. However, the money had disappeared. After examining several others, I found the money to be missing from them all. Apparently, thousands of dollars had just vanished.

Although D'Artois may or may not have removed the money from the envelopes, he certainly was responsible for the safekeeping of the records. More than likely, someone spread the money around, but no one knows for sure. And, no one in the police department wanted to talk to me about it.

As I sifted through the evidence in the vault, someone snitched on me to the commissioner. He ordered Sergeant Gullion to escort me out of the vault and not to let me in there again. He also severely reprimanded Major Justice for letting me in the evidence room.

According to Burns, once the articles started appearing in the *Times,* the police department was split wide open.

"He [D'Artois] had a lot of supporters who didn't believe what they were reading," Burns said. "But there were several of us who made up our minds to take a stand."

In an effort to protect himself during the investigation, Burns kept records of everything the commissioner ordered him to do in a safety deposit box.

Meanwhile, the Southern Research investigators, hired by Commissioner Burton, completed their probe into the funds paid to confidential informants and certain other matters. Loy Weaver, president of the company and a former FBI agent, threw a bombshell into the *Times'* investigation when he said D'Artois had supplied his men with signed receipts for more money paid to informants during 1975 than the commissioner had drawn from the city treasury to pay the informants.[8]

When asked if he could guarantee the authenticity of the documentation, Weaver said, "No, I cannot."[9] Although Weaver said his investigation was inconclusive, it appeared that D'Artois was able to account for all the funds received from the city and that the *Times'* articles about the informants' pay were in error.

The next day when I went to city hall, Captain Burns told me a bizarre story. After Commissioner Burton asked Southern Research to look into the confidential informants' payments, D'Artois called several people to his office on Saturday morning to forge the signatures of certain known confidential informants and others living just outside the law.

"They all sat around a table and George gave each one of them a pen and a receipt book and a list of names," Burns said.

Burns pointed out that the commissioner even told them the dates to write on the signed receipts. According to Burns, those who signed the bogus informant receipts were Detective Leemon Brown, his brother James Brown, a police informant by the name of Albert Richmond, and a woman by the name of Lillie Mae Hayes.

Within a couple of hours, D'Artois had hundreds of false receipts of funds that were supposed to have been given to informants. The officers did their job very well for, as Weaver pointed out, there were receipts for more money than D'Artois had received from the city. There never was any explanation as to the source of the additional funds. Some time later, both Brown and Richmond admitted before the grand jury that they were two of the people who had been called to D'Artois' office to sign the false receipts.

The false receipts ostensibly were for the year 1975. However, an examination of several of the receipts by the FBI crime laboratory in Washington, D.C., revealed that the ink in the pens used to sign the receipts was a new ink that was not on the market until sometime in 1976. Through the ink samples, they were able to determine that all of the receipts were forged, which was another felony offense.

As more stories of the commissioner's questionable activities were reported in our newspaper, a number of the city's business and political leaders told Mayor Allen to clean up the D'Artois mess. In response, he announced that he would present a resolution at the city council's next meeting calling for an investigation of D'Artois and the police department by his office and the council.

That day the mayor and D'Artois gave the people of Shreveport a lesson in Louisiana politics that even Huey Long would have been proud of. The mayor planned to let D'Artois participate in his own investigation! The commissioner told the *Journal* he planned to vote for the mayor's resolution at the next council meeting, which came as a surprise to no one.

Although Public Works Commissioner Don Hathaway said he would vote for the resolution, he would have preferred that some outside agency, the Caddo Parish district attorney, or even the state attorney general, conduct the investigation. Hathaway had served on the city council for a number of years, and he knew that D'Artois controlled the mayor and the investigation was a farce.

"Questioned about the propriety of the city investigating the city, [Finance Commissioner] Burton said, 'There is some value in showing that you can handle your own problems. Although I don't know that we really have a problem,'" the *Journal* reported.

Everyone knew that Burton was an honest man, and, like Hathaway, neither the mayor nor D'Artois told him what to do. Nevertheless, as for most of the people of Shreveport, it took time for him to grasp the depth of the corruption surrounding D'Artois. Thus, he remained in denial for a long time.

"What's going on now is devastating to the city's image," Burton told the *Journal*. "I will favor anything that brings some final disposition to this matter.[10]

"The city cannot move on anything until this is cleared up. We couldn't pull a public election right now endorsing motherhood."[11]

D'Artois really believed he had everything going his way, telling the *Journal* he was not upset by the mayor's decision for the city council to investigate his department for he knew in the end he would be vindicated.

Soon after he announced the investigation, the mayor removed both Chief Kelley and Chief of Detectives Lanigan from the probe of the police department because he and D'Artois knew they could not control them.[12] The mayor, who passed over a number of ranking police officers, chose Lt. Dan Coker to lead the investigation and detectives Bill Burson and Bill Strange to assist him.

We later learned that D'Artois recommended Lieutenant Coker. However, they made a big mistake by naming Burson and Strange to the investigation for both of them were very close to Lanigan.

From the very beginning, the investigation was a farce reminiscent of a silent movie episode of the *Keystone Cops*.

"Not only was D'Artois the police official who informed the three detectives that they would be investigating D'Artois, but the men on several occasions . . . closeted themselves with D'Artois, the man they were supposed to be investigating," the *Times* reported. "As the day went on, it became more and more apparent that D'Artois planned to play a leading role in his own investigation."[13]

From that day forward, Kelley, Lanigan, Burns, and others secretly informed me of every move the commissioner made. With Detective Burson keeping Lanigan up to date on everything that transpired in the investigation, there probably never was a reporter who had such a network of sources in any investigation of public corruption.

However, during all of their interdepartmental maneuvering on May 13 and 14, the mayor and commissioner had no idea the enterprise team was working on another story that would further shake the foundations of the power structure at Shreveport City Hall and question the activities of the lions of power.

CHAPTER EIGHT

A New Twist, a Big Surprise

The continuing saga of the rise and fall of George D'Artois as chronicled in our paper stunned Mayor Allen and the other members of the city council. In spite of these revelations, for the next few weeks, the mayor remained a staunch supporter of the embattled commissioner. He even attended barbecue and beer parties at the D'Artois home with selected police officers known to be loyal to him. I called those the "Days of Wine and Four Roses."

Sergeant Gullion, who attended one of the parties, told me, "Houn [Calhoun Allen] can really get down!"

I took that to mean the mayor lost some or most of his inhibitions after a couple of drinks. It didn't surprise me. I had written a story about a police officer in a black and white who had detained him and Public Utilities Commissioner Bill Collins late at night for urinating in the middle of the street in West Shreveport.

All politicians have a core group of people who advise them on certain matters. As we published new and incriminating stories each week in our newspaper, I believe the mayor's friends told him it was time to back away from his defense of D'Artois and stop criticizing the newspaper for its articles. Little by little, we saw his support for the commissioner fade away.

On Monday, May 17, the city council chambers were packed as the mayor and three other council members entered and were seated. The mayor, looking tired and worn out, with heavy circles under his red eyes and a troubled countenance, opened the meeting with a surprise. He was turning the entire investigation of the commissioner over to Louisiana attorney general William "Billy" Guste, Jr. of Baton Rouge.[1]

He then issued an order that no city official or employee of the city would participate in the investigation unless asked to do so by Guste or members of his staff. That order, in effect, restricted the men D'Artois had chosen to conduct the investigation from any further involvement in the sordid, criminal activities surrounding the commissioner. The mayor also said he had asked D'Artois to take a leave of absence pending completion of the investigation. However, he said the commissioner refused and planned to return to his office after his release from the hospital.

As the evidence against D'Artois mounted, a beleaguered Mayor Allen called for the commissioner to take a leave of absence until the investigation was completed. (Courtesy LSUS Archives—Noel Memorial Library)

Allen told all those present that an independent investigation by Guste's office would be the best way to handle the problems they were facing at city hall. He explained that he had proposed his own investigation before he learned that the attorney general was willing to take complete charge of the probe into D'Artois' affairs. Allen then introduced a resolution calling on all city officials and other employees to cooperate with the attorney general and his men. The resolution passed by a 4 to 0 vote.

The mayor also announced that R. M. Black of the attorney general's office would lead the investigation, along with investigators Damien Mixon, Jr. and Ben Gibbons. Allen pointed out that all of the evidence already accumulated in the investigation had been turned over to these men.

He added that the documents related to the $3,500 check earmarked for Leslie from city funds were locked in his safe over the weekend and would be given to the new investigators. For the duration of D'Artois' illness, he would personally direct the affairs of the public safety department, which also included the fire department and traffic engineer's office. Chief Kelley and Chief of Detectives Lanigan would continue to lead the police department.

"I assure the citizens of Shreveport that I am doing everything in my power as mayor to bring any possible wrongdoing or irregularities to light," Allen said. "If it should later appear that any additional offices or agencies . . . should be brought into the matter, I shall make such a request without delay. For the good of the city, these matters must be put behind us."[2]

With Mayor Allen's defection from the D'Artois camp, the commissioner's empire at city hall began to crumble. After the council meeting that morning, the defiant commissioner issued another statement from his hospital room, saying he would not take a leave of absence, as the mayor had requested but, upon his release from the hospital, would continue his leadership of the police and fire departments.

A few days later, we learned from Commissioner Burton that five more men from the attorney general's office had arrived in

Shreveport to assist Black, Mixon, and Gibbons. Most of the men, according to Burton, were accountants who would be looking into all of the police department's financial transactions for the past several years.

We also learned that Walter Smith, head of the criminal division in the attorney general's office, was in Shreveport. When J. L. Wilson and I interviewed him, he said he was in the city to check on his men's progress.

In other developments, Caddo Parish District Attorney John Richardson announced he would convene a grand jury on June 7. He indicated that if the probe at city hall should merit grand jury action, the information made available to his office would be turned over to that jury. If necessary, a second grand jury would be impaneled later to hear all the evidence concerning the irregularities in the public safety department.

Mayor Allen told me later he would ask Attorney General Guste if the city council had the authority to force D'Artois to take an involuntary leave of absence.

"Mayor Allen also said that the attorney general has full authority to bring charges against D'Artois since he is the chief investigative officer in the State of Louisiana," J. L. Wilson and I reported.

Public Works Commissioner Hathaway, who through the years had often opposed both Allen and D'Artois in the city council, said he had mixed feelings as to whether D'Artois should be forced to take an involuntary leave of absence during the investigation.

"I really don't think it makes any difference," Hathaway said. "I think the attorney general's office is going to conduct an effective investigation whether Commissioner D'Artois is in his office or not."[3]

However, Hathaway said that if D'Artois did step down, it would send a message to the public that the investigation would be free of any pressure from his presence."And it certainly would free the commissioner from any other criticism during the investigation," he continued.

Politics didn't seem to be much fun anymore for Mayor Allen, and city affairs were going down hill fast. He seemed genuinely shocked when he read the story I wrote about how the attorney general's men also planned to investigate his office and the public utilities department for possible wrongdoing. The mayor knew he couldn't justify all the charter flights he had taken at taxpayers' expense, and he had no records to prove the charter flights were related to city affairs.

"We will look into anything that appears to need investigation," Black said. "We're getting good cooperation from the people at City Hall and so far they've given us everything we've asked for."

Black told me the number of investigators from Baton Rouge had increased to fourteen men, including accountants as well as crime lab experts. I also learned that the attorney general's men had taken typing samples from the various typewriters in D'Artois' office to determine which typewriter was used to alter the invoice from Leslie.

"When we complete the investigation and finish the report, copies will be given to both the attorney general and the district attorney," Black said.

Meanwhile, Walter Smith stated, "If criminal acts are found, [District Attorney] Richardson would then present the information to a grand jury which would decide whether any indictments should be issued."

Smith added that the public would not learn of any specific charges, if there were any, against D'Artois until the charges went to the grand jury and indictments were returned.

In the midst of the investigation, Jim Montgomery wrote an editorial entitled "Shreveport's Finest" in which he paid tribute to the fine men and women of the police department.

The editorial was an attempt to reassure the police officers that the *Times* had no argument with them whatsoever and complimented them on the fine job they were doing for the citizens of Shreveport. Here is the editorial in its entirety.[4]

The phrase "Shreveport's Finest" has never been truer nor more appropriate than it is right now in describing the men and women of this city's police and firefighting forces—the people of the public safety department who, despite the turmoil surrounding Commissioner George D'Artois, have been on the job night and day as guardians of the city's welfare and safety.

From patrolmen and firemen to captains, majors and chiefs, they have worked valiantly through the disturbing atmosphere that has risen around investigations of Mr. D'Artois' questionable actions as commissioner, just as they should. The discredit Mr. D'Artois has brought upon himself does not reflect on them; they have a job to do, no matter who is commissioner, and they are doing it, as always, with high competence.

We saw them yesterday, just as we will no doubt see them today, apprehending those who violate the law, giving a friendly push to a motorist whose car had stalled, checking out the smoke in a house, investigating cases, directing traffic—doing the hundred and one things, large and small, an officer of the law or a fireman can expect to do in the course of a day's work.

In this, they are demonstrating a clear understanding of what their jobs are and where their responsibilities lie. The people of Shreveport look to them for order and assistance, and their duty is to the people. This is a relationship that stands, shining, outside and apart from the swirl of suspicion that is Mr. D'Artois' own doing.

Lack of confidence in Mr. D'Artois—who has refused to take a leave of absence even though Mayor Calhoun Allen requested that he do so during the Louisiana Attorney General's investigation into his conduct—will continue to be a millstone for the whole city so long as he remains in office, but lack of confidence in him has in no way diminished our confidence in the people of the public safety department.

Good cops and good firemen are to be treasured in any city, and we here in Shreveport have a lot to treasure. They are, indeed, "Shreveport's Finest."

On Wednesday, May 19, D'Artois launched a counterattack against the *Times* from his hospital room at Schumpert Medical Center.

"Public Safety Commissioner George D'Artois, beleaguered by charges about his official conduct and in apparent ill health, began a counterattack against his accusers today," wrote Alan Stonecipher of the *Shreveport Journal.* "D'Artois, who remained in Schumpert Medical Center this morning, authorized a statement by his personal attorney labeling the charges against him as inferences, vicious innuendo and irresponsible speculation."[5]

Stonecipher noted that two other groups echoed the theme in defense of the commissioner: "One, calling itself 'Concerned Citizens for a Better Shreveport,' distributed flyers in several neighborhoods charging the news media with using 'guilt by association' to impugn D'Artois."

In addition, Johnny Bright, president of the Central Trades & Labor Council of Shreveport, issued a statement that called on the news media "to get back to reporting business as usual instead of implying Shreveport is a corrupt city."

D'Artois' attorney, James Thornton, called a news conference that Wednesday morning to defend his client. Thornton accused the *Times*' publisher, Howard Bronson, and editor, Raymond McDaniel, of having a personal vendetta against D'Artois. He said it related to an application of the Athena Corporation for a cable television franchise in Shreveport. He noted that both Bronson and McDaniel had a financial interest in Athena, but D'Artois had voted to give the franchise to another company.[6]

The two men "may be too personally involved and perhaps too much interested in punishing those who have refused to dance to the tune of *The Times*," Thornton remarked. He went on to say that D'Artois had done some special favors for several of the owners of the *Times* but, when questioned, refused to specify how he had helped them. Thornton continued with the following:

> The plain fact is that stripped of inferences, vicious innuendo and irresponsible speculation, *The Shreveport Times* has uncovered no evidence of wrongdoing by Commissioner D'Artois. The commissioner does not ask for the citizens of Shreveport for their undying loyalty. He simply asks that he be treated with fairness and that the people withhold judgment until all the facts are in.
>
> We have every confidence that the attorney general's investigating team will investigate all the charges and will interview his witnesses before final conclusions are formed. This investigating technique will constitute a welcome contrast to the procedures employed by *The Shreveport Times*."[7]

On May 23 in the Sunday edition, editorial writer Jim Montgomery answered some of Thornton's charges.[8]

> Shreveport Public Safety Commissioner George D'Artois' mid-week statement concerning *The Shreveport Times* was a joke and has in no way deterred *The Times* from its investigative examination of Mr. D'Artois' questionable activities.
>
> Mr. D'Artois, who was still hospitalized for observation, had a six-page statement issued in a press conference by attorney James Thornton. In it, *The Times* was charged with dealing in 'inferences, vicious innuendo and irresponsible speculation.' We beg to differ. In our recent series of news stories, we have published only that which we could prove as fact. Had we been less scrupulous with fact, we could have published a great deal more than we already have.
>
> *The Times* is cooperating with investigators from the attorney general's office who are now working in City Hall. We have turned over to them a substantial amount of material gathered in our own investigation, including much material that has not been published in *The Times*.

We are impressed with the attorney general's investigators. We will also continue to cooperate with them in their work.

But we will not abdicate our right to report the news, nor will we abandon the people's right to know what that news is.

Montgomery then answered Thornton's allegation that the editor and publisher had some ulterior motives behind the investigation of D'Artois.

In his statement, Mr. D'Artois questioned our motives for this series. Major emphasis was placed on the fact that a cable television concern, Athena Corporation, was owned in part by *Times* president Howard Bronson, Jr. and Editor Raymond L. McDaniel, and that when Athena asked the City Council to amend a cable television ordinance in regard to consumer costs and completion date and the amendment was refused, the corporation's application to provide cable television service for Shreveport was withdrawn. . . .

That was in May of 1974. Yet Mr. D'Artois has charged that this incident is the cause of *The Times* series of reports published in May of 1976—two years later. He has labeled the reports 'a vendetta.' But *The Times* endorsed Mr. D'Artois for re-election on Aug. 4, 1974. . . .

We can assure Mr. D'Artois that had there been any 'vendetta' involved, we would not have waited two years to get around to it.

CHAPTER NINE

The Grand Jury

Dist. Atty. John Richardson, called the grand jury into session on June 6 to take up the D'Artois case. Richardson issued subpoenas for at least twenty-two people, including six *Times* reporters, in connection with the probe of the commissioner. According to my colleague J. L. Wilson, others scheduled to appear before the grand jury included Finance Commissioner Burton; Police Chief Kelley; Walter Cash, deputy chief of administration in the police department; and Jim Leslie. The investigators from the state attorney general's office were also expected to appear before the jurors.[1]

Obviously, the enterprise team's articles triggered the grand jury proceedings. The district attorney said the hearings would continue for several weeks, indicating that the probe was much deeper than most people had expected.[2]

On June 10, Attorney General Guste visited Shreveport to review the work of his investigators. During a news conference, he indicated "the investigation being conducted by my office into D'Artois' affairs may continue for several months."[3] Guste confirmed that his investigators were working closely with the district attorney's office but added, "Whether or not the grand jury will act on the matters is a decision for the grand jury itself."

His statement was another indication that the investigators had turned up concrete evidence of D'Artois' wrongdoing and he would be charged with some or all of the offenses reported by the enterprise team.

"This will not be a quickie. It will not be an investigation we can bring to a conclusion in a hurry," he said during the news conference.

Guste also refuted charges by the commissioner's attorney James

Caddo Parish district attorney John Richardson (left) discusses the D'Artois investigation with Louisiana attorney general Billy Guste. (Courtesy LSUS Archives—Noel Memorial Library)

Thornton that his investigators were harassing and intimidating certain Shreveport police officers, saying, "The charges are unfounded in every respect."[4]

Meanwhile, Chief Kelley said he had heard no complaints from police officers concerning harassment and intimidation from the attorney general's investigators.

"The attorney general's men have a job to do and have been doing it in a professional manner," Kelley said.[5]

However, the chief told me that a number of high-ranking police officers said they had received threatening phone calls from D'Artois from his hospital room.

"Several have come to me and told me that they have been harassed, them or their families," Kelley said.

Some of those officers told me the commissioner's lackeys had warned them that when he returned to his office he planned to fire them for their part in a so-called conspiracy against him.

According to Lt. Robert Merolla, the commissioner told him and several other officers "what we were going to say before the grand jury."[6]

"I'm not going to do it," Merolla replied.

D'Artois then threatened to have him killed and said, "You're either for me or against me."

"I told him, 'You better not miss the first time or your ass is grass.'"

When Merolla told the attorney general's investigators about his conversation with D'Artois, they stationed men around his Southern Hills home to protect his family. Merolla later stated that D'Artois tried to have both him and Captain Burns killed to keep them from testifying before the grand jury.

When the grand jury convened, the commissioner ordered several police officers to surround the courthouse and report to him the names of all the officers who were called to testify.

"However, when the sheriff's officers brought in Leemon Brown, George's bag man, they hid him in the back seat of their patrol car and when he completed his testimony, whisked him away from the courthouse without being seen by the D'Artois men," Burns said.[7]

I was the first *Times* reporter to appear before the grand jury, and it was the kind of experience that makes your butt pucker up tighter than a snare drum. As I walked into the grand jury room, the jurors appeared to be a rather cold, dispassionate group with expressionless faces. Perhaps that was the way they were supposed to appear to the witnesses who sat before them. Anticipation was burning a hole in my stomach as the bailiff asked me if I promised to tell the truth, the whole truth, and all that.

Asst. Dist. Atty. Albert Lutz questioned me about the pages missing from the Record of Arrest Book. I testified that I had learned from certain police officers the fact that gamblers were being arrested but their cases were never brought before the city courts, and I wanted to know why.

One of the grand jury members asked me if I had any idea who had cut the pages out of the arrest book.

Shreveport police detective Leemon Brown (center) was implicated in the theft of city funds charge against Commissioner D'Artois. (Courtesy LSUS Archives—Noel Memorial Library)

I said, "No," but added that it was obvious that the commissioner would be the only one with the authority to order the pages removed.

They were also interested in my examination of various large manila envelopes in the evidence room at the police station. I testified to having spent a couple of hours going through the envelopes and to what I discovered regarding the missing money. I also told the grand jurors that when the commissioner learned I was looking at some of the documents in the evidence room, he ordered Maj. Charlie Justice, the patrol commander, to escort me out of the area. Then he declared the room off limits to anyone from the news media.

All members of the enterprise team and court reporter Wilson also appeared before the grand jury. After only three days of hearing witnesses, the jurors indicted D'Artois for attempted felony theft of the $3,500 of city funds he tried to use to pay Jim Leslie for a personal campaign debt. It was the first indictment returned by the grand jury in the investigation of the commissioner, but it would not be the last.[8]

"D'Artois, due to his heart condition, was not subjected to the normal arrest procedure," Wilson wrote in an article on the grand jury proceedings. "D'Artois is accused of attempting to pay part of his 1974 campaign expenses with city funds through an invoice from a public relations firm. The invoice purportedly was altered to make it appear to be a bill for services to the city rather than services in D'Artois' bid for reelection."[9]

According to Wilson, most of the grand jury's first three days were spent studying evidence of irregularities in the commissioner's office that was gathered by the *Times*. They called about twenty-five witnesses, including Leslie and two of his staff members.

"It was Leslie who refused to accept a city check in payment for services his firm provided for D'Artois during the commissioner's 1974 campaign," Wilson reported. "Since Leslie refused to accept the check, the charge against D'Artois in the grand jury indictment is attempted felony theft, a crime punishable by a fine of $2,000, imprisonment for a year, or both."[10]

However, Wilson pointed out that had Leslie cashed the check, the maximum penalty for D'Artois would have been a fine of $3,000, ten years in jail at hard labor, or both.

Wilson explained that the grand jury was only in its initial stages, and when its investigation resumed, it would hear evidence being assembled by the investigators from the attorney general's office.

"More than 100 people have been interviewed by the attorney general's team of investigators and many are expected to testify," Wilson reported. "Hundreds of records and documents from City Hall also will be brought before the body as the probe continues."[11]

The grand jury was expected to be in session through most of the summer.

When asked to comment on the indictment, Leslie said, "I believe it's in the proper hands in the judicial system and will be handled in the proper manner. What else can I say?"

No one in the grand jury proceedings that day had any idea that a month later Leslie would be murdered in a motel parking lot in Baton Rouge.

Two days after the indictment, a recalcitrant commissioner was released from the hospital and returned to his office. He called a 9:30 a.m. news conference where he announced, "I have committed no crime. I am not about to resign."[12] He was confident he would be completely cleared of the charges against him

The Monday morning news conference was the first time the commissioner had met with the news media since mid-May when he was admitted to the hospital for observation for his heart condition.[13] He entered the hospital the same day the *Times* published the Jim Leslie story that led to his indictment for attempted felony theft.

"Asked whether he had discussed his decision to stay on the job with the mayor, D'Artois replied, 'I don't need to discuss it with him or anybody else—by law,'" Orland Dodson reported in our newspaper.

Attorney General Guste had ruled earlier that D'Artois could not be forced to take a leave of absence during the investigation.

The commissioner announced that he attended the early morning meeting during the patrol division's roll call "to let the men know I'm still alive."[14] Then he emphasized that the indictment against him was only a misdemeanor.

"During the press conference, D'Artois said, 'I would like to express my gratitude to the thousands of people who have expressed their confidence in me, and for their continued prayers through these trying times,'" Dodson wrote.

The commissioner believed most of the people of Shreveport were supporting him and that he "could be re-elected tomorrow, without question."

After the commissioner was indicted, he called several trusted police officers to a secret meeting in a park in the Cedar Grove area of the city. He also invited Joe Burleson, a traffic engineer.[15] Some of the officers who attended the meeting were loyal to Captain Burns and gave him a detailed account of everything the commissioner told the officers.

"During the meeting he said he was going to fire me," Burns said. "But Burleson told him he couldn't fire me."

"Why?" D'Artois asked.

"You can't touch him because he's a grand jury witness," Burleson replied.

According to Burns, D'Artois had learned that he and Chief Kelley were cooperating with the district attorney in the investigation and wanted to find a way to punish them.

"One day he walked over to the chief's office and just stood in the doorway looking at him," Burns remembered. "Kelley later told me, 'I didn't know if he was going to shoot me, or what.'"

I later learned that Chief Kelley, Captain Burns, and Lieutenant Merolla had a pact and promised to protect one another, and Kelley told me thirty years later that Burns and Merolla may have saved his life.

"I felt like my life was in danger many times," Kelley admitted. "[The] boys in the police department helped protect me."

The chief was so concerned for the safety of his family that he bought a pistol and gave it to his son Chester.

"Dad thought his life was in danger, but told me, 'Don't worry about me, take care of your mother,'" Chester Kelley told me later.

Patrol officers Cecil Carter and Rick Berry helped protect Chief Kelley during those terrible days and nights.

"Rick and I drove around the block where the chief lived, time after time, every night, all night long for a month," Carter said.

However, the commissioner wasn't the only person to become hostile after the grand jury proceedings. His wife, Billie Claire, became verbally aggressive toward the chief. "She cussed me for everything she could say," Kelley stated.

On another occasion, D'Artois' son Wendell saw Kelley and Burns outside the hospital after they had visited with his father.[16]

"He yelled at us, 'If anything happens to my dad, you two are dead men,'" Kelley told me. He replied with, "Son, you go on and take care of your father or I'm going to arrest you."

D'Artois, accompanied by sheriff's deputies, enters the Caddo Parish Courthouse after his arrest on charges of felony theft. (Courtesy LSUS Archives—Noel Memorial Library)

Meanwhile, a poll conducted by the *Journal* of more than five thousand people concluded that if D'Artois ran for reelection he would indeed win, though by a narrow margin of 2,596 to 2,579.[17] The *Journal* further reported:

> The virtual tie-vote, which included the telephone ballots of more than 5,000 readers showed a sharp division of opinion about his performance and a depth of emotional feeling both for and against the embattled commissioner who was indicted last Friday on charges of attempted felony theft of city funds and who is subject of a continuing grand jury investigation.
>
> The Sound Off ballot was prompted by a statement made by D'Artois at a Monday press conference when he told local newsmen he will not resign from office and he 'could be re-elected tomorrow.'"[18]

On Wednesday, two days after his news conference, D'Artois was booked into the Caddo Parish Jail on a charge of attempted felony theft. He was released after posting bond. Unlike most persons arrested and booked, he was neither photographed nor fingerprinted.[19]

On June 20, the *Times* once again called on the commissioner to step down from public office until the grand jury completed its hearings. Jim Montgomery's hard-hitting editorial reported, "Shreveport Public Safety Commissioner George D'Artois, returning to his office after an extended hospital stay and now under indictment, said at his press conference earlier this week that he has no intention of stepping aside. 'Why should I?' he responded. 'I'm not guilty of anything.'"

"Yet Mr. D'Artois has been indicted by the Caddo Parish Grand Jury, arrested, booked, charged with a crime, has posted bond and is now awaiting trial on a criminal charge."[20]

Mentioning several reasons why the commissioner should step down, regardless of his guilt or innocence, Montgomery wrote:

First, there is the atmosphere of doubt that has been raised by investigations into his activities and the grand jury hearings that have resulted, so far, in an indictment for attempted felony theft—a misdemeanor count only because the city check he tried to use to pay a personal debt was not cashed.

This atmosphere of doubt in connection with the person responsible for the administration of law in this community can only leave the citizens with a feeling of uneasiness.

The doubts, then will not fade away in the summer air, but will most likely be growing.

In addition to all of that, we must also note that Mr. D'Artois, for health reasons, has been away from the department a good deal of the time for the past six months. . . . Yet for all those months, operations of the Public Safety Department seem to have gone on with no great difficulty, and could continue to do so if Mr. D'Artois took a leave of absence now.

In short, there are no good reasons for Mr. D'Artois to occupy his office and its powers at this time; there are several good reasons for him not to.

Meanwhile, Alan Stonecipher wrote a compelling commentary on the subject of D'Artois, the media, and political hero worship.[21]

"Political hero worship is a hard habit to break in North Louisiana," Stonecipher began.

He thought that many people in Shreveport believed that D'Artois was "beyond reproach" even though he had been indicted by a grand jury. He continued by writing, "Americans have the right, of course, to like and to vote for whomever they choose. And the accused certainly have the right to be considered innocent until proven guilty. But because of political hero worship, the defense of accused public servants in this area always begins with an attack on the news media."

According to Stonecipher,

> The litany is familiar: the media . . . trumped up charges against D'Artois . . . [who] didn't do anything wrong. [Then, even if the commissioner is guilty of any wrongdoing,] "the good outweighs the bad, so why doesn't the media just shut up?" It's a tiresome old argument, and defenders of the press get tired of answering it. But the defense needs to be made again and again, until Americans finally obtain a glimmer of understanding of the role of the press. Reporters do not write fiction. They do not manufacture unfavorable stories about politicians. They do not rely on imagination.
>
> It does consider itself the monitor of the performance of public servants. The press does not ask Americans to convict politicians whose conduct has been questioned. We merely report the truth—as nearly as the truth can be ascertained by mortals—and offer that truth for the consideration of American citizens.

Many Americans would send a message to the media that says,

"Leave our heroes alone." Stonecipher said, "The media's response, provided by the U. S. Constitution's safeguards against a controlled press, is simple: We can't, and we won't."

On June 23, the grand jury indicted the commissioner on three additional counts of tampering with evidence seized in gambling raids by his own police officers.

"The three counts were included in two indictments returned in a partial report . . . by a Caddo Parish Grand Jury probing irregularities in D'Artois' office," Wilson reported for the *Times*.[22] "D'Artois, already under indictment on a charge of attempted [felony] theft of $3,500 in city funds, is accused in the latest indictments of ordering the removal from police records of cash and gambling paraphernalia seized as evidence in gambling raids."

One of the indictments accused the commissioner of an apparent cover-up. He allegedly ordered several police officers to place money and other gambling paraphernalia in falsified evidence envelopes to take the place of the envelopes that had disappeared. If convicted on all the charges, D'Artois could face up to four years in prison and be fined as much as $4,000.

Maj. Charlie Justice later testified at a hearing before the Municipal Fire and Police Civil Service Board that on the night of June 17 the commissioner called him into his office. They argued over what Justice would tell the grand jury about the two envelopes of money stolen from the police evidence vault. The commissioner earlier had ordered Justice and Sgt. D. C. Greene to place money into two other envelopes and return them to the evidence room. Justice also said that D'Artois asked him "to not let the *Shreveport Times* know about the evidence."

It appeared that D'Artois was going to let the dirt keep piling up until he buried himself alive.

District Attorney Richardson recommended that no bench warrant be issued for the commissioner's arrest due to his health problems. Caddo District judge John Fant agreed and asked Sheriff Harold Terry to notify D'Artois of the charges.

However, not all those who appeared before the grand jury were choirboys.

Although Capt. Billy T. Lambert's testimony before the grand jury was confidential, he later testified before the civil service board, which was an open meeting, that he was involved in the replacement of money, dice, and cards in the evidence vault of the police station. Lambert and others believed that D'Artois had personally removed the evidence when the gambling case never went to trial after the records of the arrest were destroyed.[23]

Sergeant Greene said that "to a degree" he assisted in putting the cards, money, and dice back into the evidence safe. He had also reported talking to the commissioner on the telephone several times on the night after he appeared before the grand jury.

"Greene said D'Artois wanted to know what Greene had told the grand jury," Marcia Desmond reported in the *Journal*. "Greene said he discussed the missing evidence envelopes with D'Artois and told D'Artois that he had told the grand jury the truth."

We later learned that after that exchange, the commissioner tried to find someone to kill Greene.

On July 1, the *Journal* published the results of another poll that showed support for D'Artois was gradually fading away. Apparently, most of the people of Shreveport were willing to give the commissioner the benefit of the doubt concerning the indictment for trying to steal money from the city. They believed him when he explained it was just an accounting error.

However, when it came to light that he allegedly had removed cash from various envelopes in the evidence room, cash seized by his own police officers in raids on illegal gambling games, and that several officers testified that he engineered a cover-up of the stolen money, the tide began to turn against him.

The *Journal* poll, conducted by Verne Kennedy & Associates of Alexandria, Louisiana, revealed that if D'Artois were to stand for reelection, he would lose by a wide margin.

"The poll, a telephone survey of 400 scientifically selected registered voters in Caddo Parish, indicates that only 23 percent of the voters now favor D'Artois for re-election," said Alan Stonecipher who reported on the poll. "The *Journal*'s Caddo poll also showed D'Artois with an extremely high negative job performance rating for an incumbent public official."

Stonecipher pointed out two-thirds of the respondents believed the commissioner should take a leave of absence during the grand jury investigation, and some seventy percent said they believed the news media had been fair in their coverage of D'Artois.

It was quite apparent that the people of Shreveport realized that D'Artois, the man who represented law and order in the community, was in serious trouble.

CHAPTER TEN

The Hit Man

After the assassin killed Jim Leslie, those of us involved in the investigation of the commissioner were concerned for our own safety. One evening, McDaniel called me into his office to tell me some disturbing news.

"Bill Keith, I had a call today from the police department," he said, a worried look on his face.

"Okay, what's up, Mr. Mac?" I asked.

"A police informant picked up some news in a bar over on the [Bossier City] Strip."

"Yeah?"

"Apparently there's a hit man from New Orleans in town to take you out," McDaniel said. "According to the informant, the man said he was here to kill Bill Keith and stop him from writing stories about George D'Artois."

Suddenly I was gripped by fear, the same kind of fear I experienced when I nearly fell out of a helicopter at fifteen hundred feet during a search-and-destroy mission in Vietnam during that war.

"Well, Mr. Mac, that is bad news," I said.

"So what do you want to do?" he asked. "Maybe you should take your family and get out of town and give the police some time to pick up this man, whoever he is."

My mind was whirling at warp speed as I tried to analyze what was happening and put the pieces of the frightening puzzle together. I had known for several weeks that there was a connection between D'Artois and Carlos Marcello.

A few weeks earlier, Asst. U.S. Atty. Graves Thomas, who later became one of Shreveport's best-known criminal defense attorneys, had leaked a copy of a confidential FBI report to my friend and

127

colleague J. L. Wilson, who made a copy of the report for me. The document told of a secret meeting in December of 1974 between an unnamed man sent by D'Artois and two of Carlos Marcello's lieutenants from New Orleans. They met in a private room at Ernest's Restaurant in Shreve Square on the Riverfront. Taking in nearly two billion dollars a year, Marcello ran the New Orleans underworld operations for nearly a half-century until his death on March 3, 1993, at the age of eighty-three. Some observers believe that Marcello's death ended the "Godfather Era" in the United States.

Although the report did not name the two men from New Orleans, it said the purpose of the meeting was to map out the mob's takeover of various illegal operations in Shreveport, including gambling, prostitution, numbers, and slots and payoff pinball machines.

The D'Artois/Marcello relationship may have dated back to the time when payoff pinball machines were running wide open in Shreveport. Although I have not been able to establish a direct connection between Marcello and the pinball machines, it is common knowledge that during that period he controlled most of the pinball and slot machines throughout Louisiana and several other states. And there is some indication the machines in Shreveport were tools of organized crime.

Even though the meeting took place at Ernest's Restaurant, there was never any indication that Ernest Palmisano, the owner of the restaurant, or any of his family members were involved in any way with the secret meeting.

If, in fact, D'Artois planned to join forces with Marcello, and provide protection for the illegal operations in Shreveport, it would have been a North Louisiana/South Louisiana criminal alliance that would have made the commissioner a very wealthy man.

Captain Burns also believed there was a D'Artois/Marcello connection and alluded to the meeting at Palmisano's restaurant. Burns said that if our newspaper had not run the stories on the commissioner and corruption in the police department, he was confident organized crime would have moved into the city.

Through the years, I've wondered why a hit man would be speaking so freely in a Bossier Strip bar. Perhaps he had too much to drink and was trying to impress one of the hostesses or the bartender. Moreover, it didn't make any sense that the commissioner wanted to have me killed. The enterprise team, through a brilliant series of stories, already had exposed his pattern of graft and corruption.

I concluded that since I wrote stories nearly every day about the commissioner, and maintained a much higher profile at city hall than the enterprise team members, he decided to have me hit and called on his friend Marcello to get the job done for him. Perhaps by killing me, D'Artois and/or Marcello would be sending a message to the editors of the *Times* that would cripple or even stop the investigation.

Why did they want me off the case? Was it for revenge?

I knew there was the possibility that Marcello had been reading the articles and watching the controversy surrounding the commissioner in Shreveport and ordered the hit himself. Maybe he thought my death would protect his planned future interests in the city and, at the same time, scare the news media away from investigating the commissioner.

Fear introduces a man to himself, and I had a grand introduction that evening.

"No, Mr. Mac, I don't want to run. If he wants me, he can find me," I said, deciding to stick around and see how it all played out.

"Okay, it's up to you, but we will take some precautions to protect you and your family," he said. "I'm going to ask the sheriff to send a deputy to escort you home tonight and also to provide you with a hand-held radio so you can contact his department any time, day or night. And tomorrow, I'm going to talk to Southern Research about some additional protection."

McDaniel never told me who called him from the police department, and I never asked.

I was nervous as the security guard opened the door and I stepped out the back entrance of the newspaper building that evening. I wondered if a sniper, perhaps the hit man from New Orleans or a fanatical friend of the commissioner, would be lurking on the roof of one of the nearby buildings or hiding in a parked car.

During the early days of the investigation, I had received several phone calls from an anonymous caller who said, "I have a .45 automatic here in my hand, and tonight when you leave the newspaper, I'm going to blow your head off." Until that night, I had never paid much attention to the phone calls or to the frequent bomb threats that forced us to evacuate the building.

About 9:00 P.M. one evening, I received a call from a man who would not identify himself but said he wanted to talk in private.

"I have some important information about the D'Artois investigation," he told me.

"Okay, but why don't you give me your name," I said.

"No, my name's not important. I just want to meet with you this evening."

"Where?"

He suggested we meet in a rural cemetery south of Shreveport.

"I don't want anyone to see us or find out that I'm giving you any information," he said.

Is this the hit man? I wondered. Is he trying to lure me into a trap?

"No, if you want to talk to me, you can do it on the phone right now, or I'll meet you in a public place sometime tomorrow. I'm not going to meet you at the cemetery."

The man hung up the phone, and I never heard from him again.

On another occasion, I received a very disturbing telephone call from D'Artois' daughter Elaine, a teenager at the time.

"Are you the man who is writing all those bad things about my daddy?" she asked.

"Yes, I have been writing some stories about your father," I replied.

"But why are you doing it?"

I thought for a moment and felt a temporary and fleeting rush of guilt. "I know your father has some very fine qualities and you love him very much, but we are looking into some things we think he may have done that were wrong."

"Oh," she said and hung up the phone.

We were all aware of what D'Artois' wife and children were going through, and I had to remind myself that he was the cause of the pain and anguish his family faced each day as new revelations about him came to light. I never enjoyed the thought that some people might be hurt by the stories I wrote.

As I left behind the safety of the newspaper building that evening, I believed my life could be in jeopardy, and I looked to the future with fear and foreboding.

I was relieved when I saw the sheriff's deputy waiting for me not far from my Chevrolet Vega, which was parked nearby. He followed me to my home near Mooringsport on a hill overlooking the south shore of Caddo Lake and waited until I reached the front door. Then he waved goodbye and drove away.

My wife greeted me at the door, unaware of the earlier events of the evening. Nevertheless, she was curious as to why the sheriff's deputy had accompanied me home. As I walked to the bedroom to check on our children, I realized our family was facing a crisis. I sat my wife down on the couch in the living room and said, "I have some bad news."

"Oh?"

"There's a hit man from New Orleans in town, and the police believe he has a contract to kill me."

My wife turned pale and began to tremble; she asked, "When did you find out?"

"Just this evening, McD got a call from someone in the police department."

"What are we going to do and what about the children?"

"I don't know. We have some decisions to make," I replied. "Perhaps you should take the children and go stay with your folks for a few weeks."

She thought for a moment, gained her composure, and said, "No, we'll stay here and face this together and trust the Lord to take care of us."

"You're sure?" I asked.

"Yes," she said.

"Okay, we'll stay here, together."

Then I explained that McDaniel was going to talk to Joe Boddie and the guys at Southern Research on some precautions we would need to take.

"We'll probably know something tomorrow," I told her.

The next day McDaniel and I met with Boddie and Johnny Pernici, a former Caddo Parish sheriff's detective and a senior operative with Southern Research. They outlined a plan to protect me and my family, a plan I later learned cost the newspaper thousands of dollars.

"First, we need to set up a silent alarm system in your house on Caddo Lake with two remotes, one for you and one for your wife," Boddie explained to me. "You can carry one in your pocket, and your wife can keep one in her purse, and you need to take them with you everywhere you go."

"How will it work?" McDaniel asked.

"When you press the button on the remote, the system will send out two silent signals—one to the sheriff's office and one to us at Southern Research," Boddie responded. "The system will be monitored twenty-four hours a day. In case of trouble, Bill or his wife will press the button and the system will kick in and send an oral message that will say, 'There's trouble at the Keith home.' The sheriff's dispatcher will contact the closest deputy who will have orders to respond immediately, and our men will be close behind."

"Okay, what else?" McDaniel asked.

"We recommend you place a half-dozen floodlights around the Keith home on the lake for additional protection at night."

McDaniel approved the recommendations, and the next day a team from Southwestern Electric Power Company began setting the electric poles. The floodlights were also installed. From that time forward, our yard was lit up like a football field at night.

The same day Southern Research technicians installed the silent alarm. My wife and I were shocked the first time the silent alarm equipment was tested. The first signal went to George D'Artois' police department rather than to the sheriff's office. I immediately called Boddie.

"How could a fool thing like that happen?" I asked him. "It's not going to do me a lot of good if I send out a distress signal and it goes to D'Artois!"

Boddie apologized, and the technicians corrected the signal.

Meanwhile, Southern Research's Pernici instructed me on matters of personal safety.

"Never take the same route home two nights in a row," he cautioned. "If you are being watched by the man from New Orleans, he will observe your movements and try to determine a pattern and then try to take you out. Also, watch for cars that are following you and those parked along the road as you return home. If you spot anything suspicious, immediately radio the sheriff's deputies."

Pernici explained that when there are two hit men working together, one will park beside the road and the other will be waiting several blocks away.

"When you pass, the guy in the parked car will radio his partner, and he will start driving toward you and will fire a couple of shotgun blasts through your front windshield," he warned.

That unnerved me. He was saying, "Be careful and be cool and you may be alive when this is all over." That night I drove home alone to Mooringsport.

Pernici suggested I call the sheriff's dispatcher each morning and night to let him know all is well. During those days of anguish, I would place Scotch tape on the doors and hood of my car to alert me if either of them had been opened. I didn't want to find out I had lost the battle after it was over.

For the first few days after hearing about the hit man, crazy thoughts ran through my mind. When I would meet a stranger on the street, in a restaurant, or at city hall, I would wonder, "Is this the man?" I often tried to imagine what such a man would look like. Later, it dawned on me that I probably would never see him, but he would see me and could be watching me every day.

There was, however, one incident of levity during the tenuous situation. Late one night, we heard a shot fired in our yard, and I immediately keyed the remote. Within two or three minutes, several sheriffs' patrol cars drove up the hill and into our yard. They drew their weapons, crouched down, and made their way across the yard, yelling to a man to drop his weapon.

Steve Moore, our neighbor, could not have been more surprised. When he saw the deputies coming toward him with drawn shotguns and pistols, he raised his hands and yelled, "Armadillo! Armadillo!" Moore explained to the deputies that he had shot a pesky armadillo in the yard.

Afterward, I learned that Sheriff Terry, who was a true friend throughout the ordeal, had instructed his men working in the northern part of the parish to make several runs by our home each night.

The owners of the newspaper also installed bulletproof windows on the west side of the newspaper building, where McDaniel's office was located. Since the building was only a sidewalk away from busy North Market Street, anyone could have thrown a bomb through the window and sped away unnoticed.

Although I had kept a double-barreled shotgun in my car for several weeks, after hearing about the hit man, I also hid a revolver under the front seat of my car. My wife carried a small automatic pistol in her purse and took it with her everywhere she went.

We received a dozen or more bomb threats at the newspaper, sometimes as many as two or three each evening. The faithful firemen, who worked for the commissioner, carefully and methodically searched the newspaper offices for bombs but found none.

CHAPTER ELEVEN

The Last Hurrah!

In other developments, on Monday, July 13, the investigation into the murder of Jim Leslie moved to Shreveport. The investigators included Detective Chris Schroeder of the Baton Rouge Police Department, Joe Folse a Louisiana State Police detective, and Harvey Blanchard of the East Baton Rouge District Attorney's Office. They met with District Attorney Richardson for more than an hour that day, discussing general background information on the Leslie case.

The investigators also met with several law enforcement agents late Monday night at an undisclosed location to discuss leads in the case. Although the FBI had not officially entered the investigation, local FBI agents also met with the investigators from Baton Rouge.

The next day Police Chief Kelley offered his assistance to the out-of-town investigators. They later met with Chief of Detectives Lanigan and Captain Burns.

The grand jury worked through the dog days of summer, and on Friday, July 24, indicted D'Artois with eight additional counts of felony theft of city funds. Once again, when asked if he planned to step down as head of the police department, he replied, "I have not been convicted of anything."[1] He wanted to study the indictments and discuss them with his attorneys before making any further statements.

The commissioner was booked into the Caddo Parish jail at 4:55 P.M. Friday about an hour and a half after the grand jury handed down the latest felony theft indictments. This time he was fingerprinted and photographed. He was released about 5:30 P.M. after posting a $16,000 bond.[2]

"The first count against D'Artois charges that between Jan. 1,

1972 and July 1, 1976, D'Artois stole $30,000 in city funds by fraudulently withdrawing said funds from the treasury of the City of Shreveport, ostensibly for the purpose of paying confidential informants for information but using said money instead for his own personal benefit," the *Journal* reported. "D'Artois could be sentenced for up to 10 years in jail if convicted on this charge."[3]

The other seven counts were for "fraudulently and falsely charging the City of Shreveport and causing to be paid by the City of Shreveport funds for charter airplane flights for personal business and pleasure."[4] Although the grand jury had indicted him on twelve counts of criminal activity, the commissioner continued to deny any wrongdoing and once again refused to resign from office.

Grand jury members also returned indictments against two police officers, Detective Leemon Brown and Patrol Captain Billy T. Lambert, for perjury. Brown was also indicted as an accessory after the fact in the theft of the $30,000.

After the last batch of indictments, we all discovered how much fight the commissioner had left in him. To punish his enemies and reward his friends, D'Artois ordered a major shake-up of the police department. He promoted Maj. Earl L. Farmer head of the Organized Crime and Intelligence Division in place of Captain Burns, who had been cooperating with the district attorney and the attorney general's investigators from Baton Rouge.

Chief Kelley objected, "I feel that any major shift should be initiated by me—or at least I should have a say-so about it."

Throughout the enterprise team's investigation of D'Artois, he maintained a defiant posture, insisting he had done nothing wrong and would be vindicated when he had his day in court. However, after the most recent indictments, the commissioner surprised everyone by suddenly resigning from office, saying his health would not allow him to continue to lead the Department of Public Safety.

"D'Artois, plagued by heart trouble and 12 charges against him by a parish grand jury, requested a medical disability retirement . . .

Shreveport Journal *reported D'Artois' resignation as commissioner of public safety.* (Courtesy LSUS Archives—Noel Memorial Library)

climaxing a three-month battle to retain his position," Stonecipher reported in the *Journal.*[5]

Mayor Allen announced the D'Artois retirement at an afternoon news conference, which the commissioner did not attend.

"Please treat this as a request that I be granted a medical disability retirement, effective this date," Allen read from a letter submitted by D'Artois to the board of trustees of the Shreveport Employees Retirement System.

Those of us who were present for the announcement were stunned yet relieved that the commissioner, who had brought such disgrace to himself, his family, and the police department, was finally out of office.

District Attorney Richardson said D'Artois' retirement would have no bearing on the criminal charges against him. Meanwhile, about two hours before the commissioner announced his resignation,

Richardson, in a very unusual move, received a restraining order from a district judge barring D'Artois from enforcing his order removing Sam Burns as head of the Organized Crime and Intelligence Division.

In response to D'Artois' retirement, Mayor Allen announced he would assume the leadership of the Public Safety Department until an election to replace D'Artois could be called. He also issued an order to reinstate Burns to his previous position.

That afternoon, I went to D'Artois' office for a final interview but learned he had left city hall through a back entrance about 5:30 P.M., thus ending the long and tumultuous career of Shreveport's top law enforcement officer.

I then spoke with Attorney General Guste, who vowed to continue his investigation into the allegations of the commissioner's wrongdoing. He told me that after conferring with Richardson, they had decided to proceed with the Leslie-related indictment of D'Artois without Leslie's testimony. The attorney general also said he would not recall his men from Shreveport until the investigation was completed. He planned "to push the case to the limit."

The day after D'Artois announced his resignation, Stanley Tiner, the *Journal* editor, wrote a very moving analysis of the man and his stormy political career. The article reflected on the political atmosphere in the city that would allow a man like D'Artois to exercise almost absolute authority.

> Like other men who have held great power . . . D'Artois seems smaller at the point of his political destruction than he should, even as he was larger than he should have been at the prime of his influence.
>
> He has been left a sad, tragic and pitiable man by his fall, and yet he surely holds the accountability for the actions of his life in public office and that accountability must yet be required of him in the courts.[6]

Tiner stated that all the people of Shreveport must consider what transpired in the city, and he believed that the news media through the years had not held D'Artois accountable for his actions, confessing, "The arrogance of attitude that eventually ran Shreveport was bred by an editorial indulgence of D'Artois and his tactics." He also observed that in the aftermath of the D'Artois scandal, the city had "ground to a halt," and the police department was divided and on the "edge of chaos."

> The fine Department of Public Safety which he [D'Artois] did so much to build in his 14 years in office, he did much to destroy in the past few weeks. . . . The story of George D'Artois is as much a tale of tragedy as any in this city's history. It is a story of achievement turned to lost opportunity and finally disgrace.
>
> Out of the lessons of this tragedy must come an understanding of the mission that faces the city, and a restoration to forge a fresh start.
>
> We must start anew as a people united, today.

The grand jury continued its deliberations through the summer, and on Saturday, July 31, Richardson announced that district court hearings would begin on Monday, August 2, to hear the testimony of Albert L. Richmond, a grand jury witness in the D'Artois case.

The *Journal*'s Alan Stonecipher reported the open court hearing would pertain to Richmond's testimony concerning Detective Leemon Brown; his brother, James Brown; and Lillie Mae Hayes, who were indicted as accessories to the alleged theft of more than $30,000 in city funds by D'Artois.[7]

It became apparent during the hearing that the commissioner had been flagrantly using people almost like a god. When the court convened on Monday, Richmond testified under oath that the commissioner threatened to have him killed and dumped into the Red River if he failed to say exactly what he was told to say before the grand jury.[8]

"Commissioner D'Artois said Leemon [Brown] would put cement around my knees and dump me in the river," Richmond said in response to questions by Asst. Dist. Atty. Albert Lutz.

A known police informer, Richmond said that D'Artois coached him on his testimony, then gave him fifty dollars before the grand jury convened.

"After Richmond's testimony, Leemon Brown took the stand and testified that he received a telephone call Sunday night threatening his life if he testified today," Stonecipher reported. "Brown said the caller told him he would be shot with a rifle."[9]

Brown also said in open court that D'Artois had called him several times during the grand jury proceedings and ordered him "to keep the others in line." The commissioner apparently was referring to Richmond, James Brown, and Lillie Mae Hayes, who were indicted by the grand jury on July 22. Brown testified that one evening D'Artois came to his home, met with him and James, and asked James to sign some receipts "to get reporters off his back."[10]

Lillie Mae Hayes testified that D'Artois called her and said, "I would hate to see your body floating in the river."

Richmond stated that on a Saturday back in April, before his grand jury testimony, Leemon Brown picked him up and took him to the commissioner's office at city hall. When he arrived, the commissioner asked him to sign dozens of blank receipts for money he supposedly received for payment to confidential informants. The commissioner told him to sign the bogus receipts with several different pens and to use the name "James Murphy" on some of them. He was also to vary the way he signed his own signature on the receipts. Richmond was paid $1.25 per hour for this service.

Having served as a police informer for ten or eleven years, Richmond stated he had never received any of the money for the receipts he signed that Saturday morning.

"He further testified that on several occasions D'Artois met with him and told him to 'stick to the story' if he was subpoenaed by the grand jury," Stonechiper reported. "The 'story,' according to Richmond, was that Richmond had signed the receipts at various times."[11]

On the day he was to appear before the grand jury, he met with the commissioner, Leemon Brown, James Brown, and Lillie Mae

Hayes in the parking lot of the First United Methodist Church in Shreveport. He said the commissioner gave each of them a fifty-dollar bill and once again instructed them "to stick to their stories."[12]

After the court hearing, a bill of information was filed charging D'Artois with four counts of threatening grand jury witnesses and a warrant was issued for his arrest.[13] However, D'Artois skipped town and the next few days were filled with suspense.

Once D'Artois had been missing for twenty-four hours, Sheriff Harold Terry issued a nationwide all-points bulletin. He called on law enforcement agencies everywhere to help find the former commissioner. Sheriff Terry heard reports that D'Artois, who by then was considered a fugitive, was seen in Texas and as far away as Las Vegas. The sheriff speculated that, because of the serious nature of his jury tampering charges, which could lead to a long prison sentence, he may have jumped bail and left the country.

Sheriff Terry also knew the commissioner had close ties to various air charter services in Shreveport and that Jerry Joyner, a police lieutenant, pilot, and close friend of the commissioner, had flown him to various destinations. He realized that it was possible for D'Artois to be out of the country in hours and hiding out in a Caribbean nation or in Central or South America.

Some believed his effort to avoid arrest was the last attempt by a proud old lawman to control his destiny and skirt the laws he had sworn to uphold.

Sheriff Terry told news reporters he planned to meet with the district attorney to determine the next course of action in locating and arresting the former commissioner. He had talked to several of D'Artois' closest friends, asking for their help in finding the fugitive.

However, a few days later D'Artois called Judge John Fant in Shreveport and informed him he and his family were in San Antonio, Texas, on vacation. He told the judge he was on his way back to Shreveport and asked him to cancel the nationwide all-points bulletin.[14] Judge Fant, unable to cancel the APB, advised him to turn himself in to the nearest law enforcement officers there in Texas. But the former commissioner refused, and the next day returned to Shreveport, ending the two-day search.[15]

Sheriff's deputies were standing by to arrest him when he arrived back in the city and booked him on four charges of intimidation of grand jury witnesses. After posting bond, he declined to speak to the reporters waiting at the courthouse.

A week later, he appeared before Judge Fant and was arraigned on seven counts of felony theft, four counts of public intimidation, three counts of destroying public records, and one count of attempted felony theft. The former commissioner pled not guilty to all charges. After the hearing, he left the courtroom on a jail elevator to avoid the newspaper reporters and television camera crews waiting for him at the entrance to the building.[16]

All of the grand jury members who indicted the commissioner were in the courtroom to observe the proceedings.

CHAPTER TWELVE

Tales of Treachery and Intrigue

Early in September there were numerous stories of treachery and intrigue—and new developments in the investigation into the murder of Jim Leslie—which all of us at the *Times* followed with great interest.

A retired detective named John Templin, in a voluntary deposition, told Baton Rouge detectives that D'Artois asked him to kill Leslie. The *Baton Rouge Morning Advocate* reported that Templin visited D'Artois at Schumpert Medical Center on May 26, 1976. At that time, he said the commissioner told him, "There's something I need done. I need for you to take care of Jim Leslie."

In the deposition, which apparently was leaked to a *Morning Advocate* reporter, Templin quoted the commissioner as saying, "I need for you to go to him, put him in your car and get rid of him. Do something with him. He don't have to be found, ever, just disappear."[2]

Templin attended high school with the commissioner, and they had been good friends through the years. "He [D'Artois] has always been my hero—someone to look up to, someone to admire. But this has torn me apart."[3]

According to the *Morning Advocate,* when Templin refused to kill Leslie, the commissioner asked him who would do the job, and he mentioned the name Clifton Guevara. After Templin heard the news report that Leslie had been killed, he reported his conversation with the commissioner to the FBI.

Templin later said he felt threatened by the disclosure of his conversation.

"This is real premature and I think it puts me and my family in a kind of dangerous position," he said from his home in Deadwood, Texas, where he lived at the time.[4]

The request for him to kill Leslie left him in shock, saying such a request "would shock anyone, if the offer was made to anyone that had any morals at all."

The day before we learned about Templin's deposition, Caddo Parish sheriff's deputies, with a warrant issued by the East Baton Rouge Parish authorities, arrested Guevara on a charge of armed robbery. They also planned to question him in the Leslie murder.[5] Guevara and three other assailants had allegedly robbed two Baton Rouge men of the $12,800 they had won at a New Orleans racetrack.

"The warrant charges Guevara with two counts of armed robbery, one count of aggravated burglary and one count of attempted murder in connection with a holdup in Baton Rouge last December. Release bond was set at $115,000," J. L. Wilson and John Hill reported in the *Times*.[6]

If convicted, Guevara, who had been arrested several times on various charges and had already served time in prison, would face a possible 297 years in prison.

"Guevara, in handcuffs, was immediately whisked to the Downtown Airport here where he boarded a state police helicopter for the trip to Baton Rouge," Wilson and Hill reported. "He was accompanied by Sgt. Chris Schroeder of the Baton Rouge police and State Trooper Jimmy Harrel, both of whom have been active in recent weeks in the investigation of Leslie's death."[7]

According to the reporters, when Guevara arrived in Baton Rouge, he was wearing a body chest strap with his handcuffs attached and was hurried to a waiting police car and transported to the Baton Rouge police station.

Meanwhile, Walter Monsour, chief assistant district attorney of East Baton Rouge Parish said the arrest of Guevara "was not due to the Leslie case, but it would be ludicrous for me to say we don't intend to question him about the Leslie murder, because his name has been so prominent in intelligence reports on the investigation."[8] Monsour added that Guevara "is known to have visited D'Artois in the hospital prior to Leslie's murder."

Guevara did admit to having been asked by D'Artois to "get rid of" Jim Leslie. However, after further questioning by the authorities, they found no firm connection to the Leslie murder. Baton Rouge chief of police Howard Kidder concurred that Guevara was not involved in the Leslie killing but said, "We are making progress on the Leslie case."[9]

Several months later, Guevara's attorneys Graves Thomas and Mike Maroun of Shreveport told a district court in Baton Rouge that D'Artois asked their client several times to kill Leslie before the advertising executive was murdered by a shotgun blast in July.[10] The attorneys also alleged that D'Artois asked their client to kill two Shreveport police officers, Capt. Sam Burns and Sgt. D.C. Greene, before they would have a chance to testify before a Caddo Parish grand jury.[11] They further stated their client had passed a polygraph test, which cleared him of any involvement in the Leslie murder.

I found it quite interesting that Guevara could afford an attorney like Maroun, who had served as Carlos Marcello's attorney for some twenty-five years, and I never quite understood the connection with Guevara.

In another episode of the commissioner's treachery and intrigue, Maj. Charlie Justice testified before the Municipal Fire and Police Civil Service Board that on the night of June 17, D'Artois pulled a gun from his desk and threatened his life if he told what he knew about missing police evidence to the grand jury.

I felt a lot of sympathy for the major during the hearing. He appeared nervous and about ready to go over the edge at any time. He was the kind of guy who was in such a hurry and so stressed out that I felt like I had a dose of caffeine just looking at him.

As a patrol major, he was responsible for the Record of Arrest Book. Therefore, he was in big trouble with the commissioner after I discovered the missing pages. He also authorized the desk sergeant to let me look through the files in the evidence room, making the commissioner so mad he threatened to kill him.

I remember one day when I walked into the men's restroom at the police station. Justice was facing a urinal and when I said hello he jumped as if he had just heard the devil call his name. He had an anemic, wan complexion and was so scared he stopped in midstream and hurried out the door so fast I'm sure he soiled his underwear. Like a number of other police officers, he didn't want to be seen talking to me, even in the toilet.

Justice reported that on the night of June 17, D'Artois called him to his office where they argued over what he would tell the grand jury about money stolen from several envelopes in the evidence room. He said D'Artois ordered him and Sergeant Greene to replace the money originally enclosed in the envelopes. The commissioner also told him not to let any of the *Times'* reporters know about replacing the evidence.

However, I already knew about the missing funds and had written a story about them.

According to Justice, the commissioner was crazy mad that evening. "D'Artois pulled out his gun twice. He pulled out the gun, and it had a big barrel on it."

Justice told the hearing that about that time Captain Lambert came into the office and, when he saw Justice, said, "What you need is one of these pills." However, Justice did not say what kind of pills they were.

"After the commissioner got through with me I took the pills and you would have too if your life had been threatened," Justice confessed.

That night, after he returned home, Justice received a phone call. The caller warned him that if he testified before the grand jury, he would get his head blown off. Although he could not identify the caller, he thought it was strange that the call came right after the commissioner had threatened him.

Lambert said that later Justice told him if the information about the stolen evidence being returned to the vault became public knowledge, "he would be hurt."

During a pretrial hearing at the Caddo Parish Courthouse,

Detective Brown testified that D'Artois ordered him to kill a black man by the name of Sterling Sneed, a known gambler in the city. (Sneed was one of ten men arrested in July of 1976 in a gambling raid, but he never appeared in court.) Brown said the commissioner called him to Schumpert Medical Center in May when he was a patient and ordered the murder.[12] The commissioner did not explain to him why he wanted Sneed dead.

"He asked me did I know a fellow named Sterling Sneed," Brown said. He identified him as a black gambler who lived at 1531 Buena Vista and "told me to go and kill him and leave him where he wouldn't be found."[13]

Brown was afraid that D'Artois, a heart patient, was going to have another heart attack if he refused.

"I said, 'Commissioner, do you realize I'm a police officer?' He looked at me and said, 'Leemon, a police officer is the easiest man in the world to kill. Now you take care of this.'"

The commissioner called Brown after he returned home and once again ordered him to kill Sneed, ordering, "Take care of it . . . take care of it tonight."

After that, D'Artois called the detective to his hospital room every day, and when he arrived, he always asked everyone else to leave the room. Then he asked him once again to kill Sneed.

"Go out there and get him and be sure you put him where he won't be found," Brown said the commissioner told him.[14]

Brown finally made up his mind to tell D'Artois he was not going to kill Sneed. The next day, he went to the hospital to see the commissioner and told him, "Don't ask me [to kill anyone] again."

Mayor Allen called a special election for October of 1976 to replace D'Artois as commissioner of public safety. Chief Kelley was one of the first to announce his candidacy for the office.

Since I had firsthand information on the role Kelley played in bringing down Commissioner D'Artois and exposing graft and corruption at city hall, naturally I wanted him to be the next commissioner.

During a meeting of the West Shreveport Association, Kelley candidly spoke of his role in exposing D'Artois. When he learned D'Artois was stealing money from the city and taking payoffs from bar and nightclub owners, he went to the *Shreveport Times* and relayed what he knew to the editor and publisher.

"I had nobody else to go to so I went to the newspaper," Kelley said.[15] "I accepted my responsibility and I did my job." He added that D'Artois was forced to resign because "a group of policemen did their job, and I was part of that group."[16]

In a related story, the *Journal* noted that for the first time since 1962, D'Artois would not be on the ballot as the people of Shreveport chose a new public safety commissioner.[17]

"But the legacy of the discredited former commissioner, who resigned during the summer after several indictments, will still be a factor in the special election," Alan Stonecipher reported.[18]

Stonecipher pointed out that there were thirteen candidates in the race who were not only running against each other, but also against the record of the D'Artois administration.

"For T. P. Kelley, that record provides both an advantage and a disadvantage," Stonecipher said.[19]

Kelley served under D'Artois for five years after he was named chief of police in 1971. Political and civic leaders believed that because of his long and successful career with the FBI, he would keep D'Artois honest or at least blow the whistle when something went wrong.

"So when the public safety scandals erupted this year, the question arose: Where was Kelley?" Stonecipher asked.[20]

Kelley answered that question by saying he was notifying the newspaper about his suspicions and cooperating with the grand jury. This information led to the newspaper's exposé and the grand jury indictments.

The *Times* endorsed Kelley for commissioner and, in an editorial, said, "Make no mistake about it, had it not been for T. P. Kelley, there would have been no exposé of the gross corruption in the public safety department, and that corruption would no doubt be continuing even today."[21]

Terry Hayes, a former firefighter, won the race. Kelley, who finished second, opened his own private investigation firm. Hayes was really a breath of fresh air. He was an honest, sincere, hardworking public servant who restored pride and morale to the police department. Law and order returned to the department and to the city after many years of corruption under the leadership of D'Artois.

A short time after he was elected, Hayes named Kenneth Lanigan chief of police. Lanigan, a twenty-seven-year veteran, became the first police officer to rise through the ranks to become the department's highest officer. During his career, Lanigan had solved a number of major criminal cases and had received numerous awards for his police work.[22]

In 1954, *True Detective* magazine, a national publication, named Lanigan "the toughest cop of the year" in the United States.

After the city council approved Lanigan as the new chief, he acknowledged the department's "morale problem" and promised to do his part to restore a respect for the law in the department after the recent turmoil.

"We have an outstanding police department, one of the finest in the country," Lanigan said. "But it has been lacking in leadership and direction."[23]

However, the saga of Commissioner D'Artois was a story that would not go away as further revelations of his misconduct continued to come to light.

CHAPTER THIRTEEN

The Murder of Rusty Griffith

Rusty Griffith, a Shreveport crime figure whose name appeared in several intelligence reports in the Leslie murder investigation, was lured to his own death in a midnight rendezvous in a remote area of Concordia Parish on Saturday, October 16, 1976.

The former bar owner and limousine service operator, who weighed four hundred pounds and looked like the victim of a gypsy's vengeful curse, faced his worst fears as he was killed by a double-barreled shotgun blast to his face in another gangland-style murder like that of Leslie.[1]

Baton Rouge detectives working to solve the Leslie murder moved into Concordia Parish after Griffith's body was discovered by members of the United States Army Corps of Engineers about 6:00 A.M. on Saturday in the Three Rivers Wildlife Management Area. The detectives wanted to find out if there was a connection between the two murders.

Three Rivers is an isolated area covered with bitter pecan, honey locust, nuttall oak, and bottomland hardwoods. And, with the heavy underbrush, it was the ideal setting for a clandestine meeting of men who lived outside the law. Located in the southern tip of Concordia Parish fifty miles south of Vidalia and fifteen miles north of the Louisiana State Penitentiary at Angola, Three Rivers Wildlife Management Area is between the Mississippi and Red Rivers and just north of Lower Old River.

According to Baton Rouge chief of police Howard Kidder, Griffith was in Baton Rouge the night Leslie was killed. In addition, the *Baton Rouge Morning Advocate* reported that Griffith was once an associate of Guevara, who was questioned in the Leslie murder.[2]

Sheriff Fred Schiele of Concordia Parish called the murder "a real professional job." He believed that particular location was chosen because it was so remote.[3]

Shreveport police captain Sam Burns said Griffith had been a shadowy figure around the city for several years.

"He really thought he was the godfather in Shreveport," Burns recollected.

Griffith once operated the Inside Out Club in Shreve Square and Big Daddy's Lounge on Line Avenue. His limousine service brought people from Dallas and Houston to the Louisiana Downs Racetrack in Bossier City. Before he was killed, a federal grand jury in Jackson, Mississippi, indicted him on a charge of interstate transportation of stolen merchandise, including heavy construction equipment.[4]

Sheriff Schiele said that items, including several briefcases, notebooks, and memos, found in Griffith's car included the names of a number of known crime figures thought to be connected with organized crime in Louisiana, Arkansas, and Texas.[5]

"The papers listed hundreds of names, addresses and dates. . . . Many of the names would be familiar in the Shreveport area," Schiele stated.[6]

The sheriff also said he had learned that Griffith had been under limited surveillance by law enforcement officers, from both the Shreveport and Baton Rouge police departments, who believed he may have had knowledge of who killed Leslie.

On November 8, Schiele reported that several arrests were imminent in the Griffith murder case.[7] According to him, a thirty-three-year-old Baton Rouge truck driver, Jules Ron Kimbel, was arrested after he allegedly made an anonymous telephone call to Bob Anderson, a *Baton Rouge Morning Advocate* reporter, and gave him inside information on the Griffith murder. Anderson, who recorded the conversation, gave the tape to investigators.

"He [the caller] was informed at that time that his call was being taped and his permission was received to turn the information over to authorities," Henry Delahunt of the *Journal* reported.[8]

Kimbel told Anderson he and Griffith went to the secluded area on the night of October 15 to meet two other men.

"When the car they were supposed to meet drove up, the passenger opened the window and shot Griffith twice in the face with a shotgun," the *Shreveport Journal* quoted Anderson as saying.[9]

Although he was careful not identify him, Kimbel told Anderson the driver of the car was a suspect in the Leslie murder investigation. According to Kimbel, Griffith often bragged about being a friend of Commissioner D'Artois.

Baton Rouge authorities were hopeful that Kimbel could provide information about the transportation of stolen heavy equipment, drug smuggling, and the Leslie murder.

A year after Griffith was murdered, Anderson wrote a very detailed account of the murder based on interviews with Kimbel and two other eyewitnesses to the killing. (The story was reprinted with permission by the *Journal*.)

According to Kimbel's version of events, Griffith drove his brown Cadillac into the dark and wooded Three Rivers area. The trees were naked and ugly. The moon was down, it was dark, and the road was doubtful. Since Griffith was so large, he had some difficulty getting out of the front seat of his car, which served as his traveling office, complete with all kinds of records, notes, and receipts.[10]

The big man was nervous there in the dark, heavily wooded area, where faint trails sneaked off into the thick woods with tangled vines and interlocking trees and the night could seduce a man. He was more accustomed to meeting in expensive hotel rooms, but the situation had changed, and now the heat was on him. Although he had danced with the devil for years, he didn't realize it was payback time.

"For years 'Rusty' Griffith had been juggling funds, leaving a $10 tip to a barmaid one day, borrowing money the next," Anderson reported. "Alternately he operated bar rooms, a Dallas to Shreveport limousine service, a statewide seafood business, and the more lucrative, shady sidelines of each."

There were reports that some limousine services brought prostitutes into Bossier City from larger cities such as Houston and Dallas to work the Louisiana Downs Racetrack gamblers who frequented the bars and nightclubs on the Bossier Strip.

"He traveled constantly with business deals from Texas to Mississippi, from Costa Rica to Mexico," alleged Anderson. "He played big money games with high rollers. He sold not only stolen heavy equipment on an international scale, but was the merchant of pleasure and dreams as well."

That night in rural Concordia Parish, Griffith was selling secret tape recordings of telephone conversations. However, the article continued, "Even today nobody knows the full contents of those recordings, though educated speculation is that they concerned narcotics deals, heavy equipment thefts and 'exports,' securities fraud and information on the Jim Leslie murder."

Griffith had already decided that night that the people who wanted the tapes would have to pay a lot of money for them. He thought the money would be enough to pay his attorneys in the upcoming federal court case and provide for his wife and children in case he was convicted and sent to prison.

He winced when he saw a set of headlights moving through the woods toward where he was standing. The lights drew closer, and he saw a pickup truck as it rounded a curve near where his Cadillac was parked. He relaxed some when he recognized the truck. It belonged to Kimbel, better known to Griffith as Ricco, a man he thought he could trust. Kimbel drove on past him and parked the truck in the woods and out of sight. Griffith knew that Kimbel was no angel, but he thought he and the dark-eyed country boy were friends. The young man was nervous as he walked through the woods and the moonless night toward Griffith, a flashlight in hand.

"Earlier in the week they had come here together, but the people they were to meet had not shown up," Anderson quoted Kimbel as saying. "They had sensed the danger then and agreed that tonight they would come separately and not let themselves become a single target in case it was guns and not money that their associates brought to the lonely meeting place."

As he approached Griffith, he switched off the flashlight, greeted the big man and told him it probably would be raining before the night was over.

There was a slight chill in the air, and the night wind had started to sing. The men could hear the buzz of mosquitoes, adding to the night sounds.

"They chatted nervously before Rusty grew serious," reported Anderson.

"Don't let them jam me up," Griffith said.

He then told Kimbel to walk on up the road and watch for the men they were supposed to meet. Griffith asked the young man to signal him with the flashlight when the others arrived and that would let the big man know that everything was all right.

It was a few minutes after 9:00 P.M. when Kimbel walked up the rutted road to where he would wait for the "friends" to arrive. He could hear the sounds of the night, the brush of leaves, and the cracking of a twig or a dry limb breaking under his feet. There was a hint of rot in the air. About forty yards up the road, he stopped and waited, all the time slapping at mosquitoes. About 9:15 P.M., Kimbel looked down the dark road and saw the headlights of two automobiles approaching. He held the flashlight tightly in one hand, a pistol in the other.

Kimbel recalled to the reporter, "One of the cars stopped, lights visible through the underbrush. Its headlights went out. The lead car kept coming." As the car approached him, he signaled with his flashlight for them to stop. "A green Torino pulled up next to him, and he directed the beam inside."

Even though Kimbel was nervous about the second car waiting down the road, he signaled Griffith with one flash of his light. He then motioned for the driver of the Torino to continue down the rutted road. Kimbel stared at the taillights of the Torino as it approached Griffith. He watched as Griffith walked up the passenger's side. He knew his double cross was just about over when Griffith leaned against the car to talk to the men.

Then he heard a scream!

"It was not a scream for help. . . . Rusty's scream was a curse, a damnation for the occupants of the green Torino into which he stared," wrote Anderson. "He died with that curse on his lips as the double blasts of the shotgun disintegrated his face."

The green Torino pulled away from Griffith's dead body and sped toward Kimbel. He motioned them on with his flashlight.

Waiting in his car near the highway, a man by the name of Steve Simoneaux, one of the conspirators, heard the shots that carried through the trees and the moist air. A few minutes later, the Torino passed him and sped away from the scene. Simoneaux followed them to the intersection where the car had stopped and let one of the men out. He picked up the man beside the road and returned to Baton Rouge.

Both Kimbel and Simoneaux were reluctant to identify the other participants in Griffith's murder.

"Other people heard the shots and saw the cars speed onto the main highway, but it was the day before hunting season opened and they figured someone had been poaching and was now fleeing a game warden," Anderson said.

Kimbel passed by Griffith's lifeless body as he returned to his pickup truck. He did not stop to look at him. He knew enough about shotguns to visualize the man's face. He then drove quickly down the rutted road as his dog cages rattled in the back of his truck.

Two days later Ricco Kimbel, apparently feeling some guilt over his betrayal of Griffith, called the *Baton Rouge Morning Advocate* and nervously related the events of that Friday night to reporter Bob Anderson.

"He did not give his name, and when he did not call back within three days as he promised, a search for him was begun by the newspaper, state police and the Concordia and East Baton Rouge Sheriff's offices," Anderson said.

They located him two weeks later through clever detective work, using his voiceprint from the recorded conversation with Anderson, and placed him under protective custody.

"A number of persons were subsequently arrested in connection with the murder, but all were later released when some provided alibis and Kimbel balked at testifying without being given immunity," Anderson said.

After questioning Kimbel for several hours, authorities became convinced that there was a connection between the Griffith and Leslie murders. With his help, investigators located two other key witnesses, Simoneaux and Clayton Kimble, Ricco's brother. (Although they were brothers, they spelled their last name differently.) At first, the men refused to testify unless granted immunity, but eventually, they obliged.

Some believed that Griffith had been killed because he had been talking to investigators about immunity for his testimony in the Leslie murder.

"If indeed Rusty Griffith was going to tell all he knew in exchange for immunity, the Leslie case and countless other criminal investigations might have been wrapped up," Anderson said. "Some important people would probably have gone to jail. Instead they took the gamble of killing the big man. What remains to be seen is whether or not that gamble paid off."

These many years later, there still are unanswered questions about the Rusty Griffith murder. But we do know his love of money was his weakness, doubt and indecision his curse, and tragedy his destiny.

Several months later, Sheriff Schiele arrested Clayton Kimble and his brother Jules Ron "Ricco" Kimbel for the Griffith murder. They were convicted and sentenced to life in prison.

"U. S. District Judge John V. Parker said the life sentences he imposed . . . on [the] two brothers were justified by the 'horrible and vicious crime' they committed which resulted in the 'cold-blooded murder' of Rusty Griffith," Nora Norris of the *Baton Rouge Morning Advocate* reported.[11]

Judge Parker called the brothers a threat to the community.

"If ever there were two people qualified to be identified as career criminals, it is you."[12]

Prior to the sentencing, prosecutors asked the judge to impose a punishment that would send the message that murder of witnesses will not be tolerated in Louisiana.

In a related matter, Steve Simoneaux, chief witness for the prosecution of Kimbel and Kimble, was sentenced to twenty years in prison for his part in the Griffith murder. He agreed to cooperate with the authorities in return for the reduced sentence.

Norris reported there was one reference to the Leslie murder in a letter to the court from prosecutor Ian Hipwell, which said in part:

"Steve Simoneaux, Clayton Kimble and Jules Ron Kimbel successfully avoided prosecution for the murder of Jim Leslie and Rusty Griffith for over five years because of police and prosecutorial ineptitude and their own cleverness."[13]

The prosecutors believed that Griffith was an accomplice in the Leslie murder and was killed to keep him silent about the case.

CHAPTER FOURTEEN

Standoff at the D'Artois Home

During the winter months, the various law enforcement agencies continued their intense investigation into the murders of Jim Leslie and Rusty Griffith. To their credit, they networked together and shared information that might be helpful in solving these two terrible crimes.

As the spring of 1977 approached, the people of Shreveport experienced a fatigue of faith as they questioned whether they would ever know who killed Leslie and Griffith. It appeared that the unsolved murders would be millstones around the necks of the people of Shreveport for generations to come.

Stan Tiner, editor of the *Journal,* wrote a column on March 18, 1977, in which he addressed this issue.

"There is a pall over Shreveport City Hall." Tiner argued. "The mood is funereal."[1]

Tiner, who at one time was a reporter for the *Times* and often covered stories at city hall, said he had never seen "such a mood of depression" as when he had recently visited Shreveport's seat of government.[2] Following D'Artois' resignation, the people of the city seemed to be lulled into a false sense of well being, and there was the general impression that the matters of concern at city hall had been cleared away.

"They have not," he said. "Many of the allegations concerning the Public Safety Department have not been dealt with and cry out for attention."[3]

April of 1977 marked the first anniversary of the enterprise team's original story on D'Artois' attempted felony theft. Most of us were concerned that he was still a free man, having never been brought to trial on any of the charges leveled against him.

However, on Monday, April 4, District Judge William Fleniken set a court date of May 2 for the D'Artois trial to begin. Once again, D'Artois' attorneys said they would appeal the ruling and continued their worn-thin argument that he was too ill to stand trial.

As I think back over his lawyers' stalling tactics, I remember the commissioner was not too sick to make midnight phones calls to Detective Brown, ordering him to kill a certain gambler in the city. He was not too sick to travel to Hot Springs, Arkansas, to gamble. He was not too sick to threaten Major Justice and wave his gun back and forth in his face. He was not too sick to threaten Chief Kelley, Captain Burns, and Lieutenant Merolla.

On the night of Tuesday, April 19, two weeks before D'Artois was scheduled to appear in court, there were some new developments in the Leslie murder investigation. It is difficult to explain how a reporter knows something big is going down; it's like an indescribable sixth sense. However, that evening both J. L. Wilson and I were convinced there had been a breakthrough in the case.

Our sources in the police department and the district attorney's office informed us that sheriff's deputies from East Baton Rouge Parish and Concordia Parish had arrived in Shreveport that afternoon. Although Wilson and I didn't know exactly why they were in our city, we guessed it had something to do with the Leslie murder.

Sheriff Schiele of Concordia, in a Monday afternoon interview, said the Griffith murder "resulted from a blackmail conspiracy involving a number of taped recordings of information concerning the Leslie murder and a blackmail plot to keep the tapes from being revealed."[4]

The sheriff told us his deputies had questioned three men who gave them detailed information about the two murders. He identified the men as Jules Ron Kimbel, Clayton Kimble, and Steve Simoneaux. He said that Simoneaux would be a state's witness in both the Leslie and Griffith murder cases since he helped arrange both executions. The sheriff also alluded to there being other witnesses who were turning state's evidence in the two murder cases.

"If it's a question of immunity . . . we will be able to give them whatever is necessary for their information," the sheriff said. "What they have given us so far through the polygraph and PSE [Psychological Stress Evaluator] has checked out correct."[5]

Then Wilson and I learned from John Hill, our capital correspondent, that a Baton Rouge television station, well known for investigations into political corruption in state government, reported that the arrest of D'Artois for Leslie's murder was imminent.

However, that was not enough for McDaniel, who had a passion for accuracy in our newspaper. As the editor, he knew that more than 100,000 people would read the *Times* the next morning. If, for any reason, the out-of-town deputies failed to arrest the commissioner, we all would be embarrassed. He told us to come up with more information or there would be no story of a pending arrest.

Wilson and I went back to work. He kept in touch with Sheriff Terry and Assistant District Attorney Lutz, and I called Chief Kelley and Chief of Detectives Lanigan. They all knew that D'Artois would be arrested the next morning, but, as professionals, they refused to break their confidence. Although they did not acknowledge the arrest, they did not deny it.

About 10:00 P.M., we got a break. Earlier we had asked John Hill to check if there had been an arrest warrant issued by a Baton Rouge judge for D'Artois' arrest. When he checked, he found there was none. However, Hill later called us to say he had a tip from a source in the clerk of court's office that the arrest warrant had been issued by the district court judge of Baton Rouge, Douglas Gonzalez, just at closing time, apparently to keep the news media from finding out. Law enforcement officers often wait until the last minute to get a warrant, particularly when they want to keep a pending arrest secret.

Later that evening, we learned that two East Baton Rouge Parish sheriff's deputies, Nick Ross and Glenn Smith, were drinking in a downtown bar, and after a few too many drinks, they told several of the other patrons that they were in Shreveport to arrest D'Artois. After we heard from Hill and confirmed the two Baton Rouge detectives were in the city, McDaniel told us to go ahead and write the story. In all my years as a journalist, the work that Wilson, Hill, and I did that night was probably the high point in my journalistic career. We experienced firsthand what all of us already knew—effective investigative reporting requires a team effort.

Our lead story the next morning simply said that law enforcement officers from East Baton Rouge and Concordia Parishes had converged on Shreveport on Monday to make a series of arrests in the Jim Leslie and Rusty Griffith murder cases and that the deputies brought with them a warrant for the arrest of D'Artois.

Before daylight on Wednesday, April 20, D'Artois unlocked the front door of his home on Ashbourne Street and walked out into

D'Artois implicated in the murder of Jim Leslie in a Shreveport Times *story. (Courtesy LSUS Archives—Noel Memorial Library)*

the yard to pick up his morning newspaper. When he opened it, he read the headline "Arrests Due Today in Two Murders; D'Artois Named."

He walked back into his house and locked the door. Thus began one of the most traumatic days in the history of the City of Shreveport.

Early that same morning East Baton Rouge Parish detectives Ross and Smith delivered a warrant for the arrest of D'Artois to Caddo Parish sheriff Harold Terry.

Sheriff Terry assigned veteran deputies J. W. Jones and Bob Teros to serve the warrant, beginning an eight-hour ordeal that Jones later described to me as "tense and dangerous and filled with constant uncertainty."[6]

The following scenario is based on my personal interview with Jones on April 11, 2006.

He and Teros, a big, strong weightlifter who weighed 220, left the sheriff's office at 6:30 A.M. and arrived at D'Artois' home at 6:50 A.M.

"The weather was clear, and it was a beautiful spring day in Spring Lake," Jones told me. "We walked up to the front door and rang the doorbell. We also knocked on the door, but no one answered. Then I called the office and asked them to call the D'Artois home and tell them we were there at the front door. I also went to the back door, and when I returned, Teros told me that George had come to the front door and looked out but did not open the door."

About ten minutes later, the commissioner's wife Billie Claire let the two deputies in through the back door.

"She told us he was not at home and that it was her who had come to the front door," Jones said.

"Mrs. D'Artois, I know George and that was him that came to the front door," Teros replied. "We have a first-degree murder warrant for Mr. D'Artois."

The arrest warrant allowed them to search the house, and as they went from room to room, Jones saw a copy of that morning's *Shreveport Times* on the kitchen table. So he knew the commissioner was well aware of why they had come to his home.

For Jones and Teros, the next hour was cloaked in uncertainty, as they could not find D'Artois anywhere in the house. While searching a bedroom, later in the morning, Jones found a hole in the ceiling of the closet leading to the attic. He looked into the attic and could tell from tracks in the dust on the beams that someone had been up there.

Jones found the commissioner's prescription glasses on one of the beams in the attic, so it was evident to him and Teros that D'Artois was hiding somewhere in the attic. The deputies finally discovered him behind several layers of fiberglass insulation. On discovery, the commissioner, breathing hard and sweating from the heat in the attic, began waving a .357 magnum, daring the men to try to arrest him.

"Mrs. D'Artois was nervous and crying," Jones said. "She urged us not to go into the attic or someone might get shot."

However, Jones called to the commissioner, told him he had a warrant for his arrest, and asked him to come on out.

"You could see his heart beating," Teros said. "It was just pounding."

"His daughters kept calling to the attic, saying, 'Daddy, come down,'" Jones recalled.

According to Jones, during the time they were trying to talk him out of the attic, he would get irritated and say, "Go back down, I don't want to talk to you anymore."

He finally agreed to come down out of the attic only if the deputies would back away and let him go into the second-floor bathroom. He also wanted a typewriter and typing paper. They granted his request.

D'Artois crawled down out of the attic and barricaded himself in the bathroom, with his gun. Some time later, he passed three or four pages under the bathroom door and asked Jones to give them to his wife and not to read them.

Billie Claire repeated to the deputies her fear that her husband would commit suicide if they cornered him or perhaps wanted one of the deputies to shoot him.

"I continued to talk to him and said we had a warrant and were just doing our job," Jones said. "This went on for several hours, me asking him to come on out and him saying he wanted to finish his work. When he finished typing, he sent eight or ten pages under the door to his wife. I gave the information directly to Mrs. D'Artois."

Meanwhile, KEEL Radio's early morning news program broke the news that the deputies had gone to D'Artois' home to serve a warrant for his arrest in connection with the murder of Jim Leslie and that the former commissioner had barricaded himself in his attic and would not surrender to the deputies. KEEL employees picked up the news on their police scanner and overheard Jones and Teros briefing Sheriff Terry on the volatile situation.

After hearing the news report, I hurried into the office from my home in Mooringsport. McDaniel told me and my partner Elaine King to take a photographer to the D'Artois home to cover the story. When we arrived, a large crowd had already gathered, including reporters from the *Journal* and various radio stations and camera crews from the three major television stations in the city.

"As the word of the incident spread, by 9:25 A.M. cars lined both sides of Ashbourne Street and crowds of news media and onlookers swarmed the neighborhood," Elaine King reported.[7] "At one point, at least 100 persons were milling around in front of the D'Artois home—just watching."

The crowd could only wait and wonder.

As soon as we arrived, a reporter from KEEL asked me for an interview since I had been involved in the D'Artois investigation for the past year. The reporter had read our story in the morning paper, and I provided background information on how J. L. Wilson and I had put the story together, saying it was evident Baton Rouge authorities had some very damaging information implicating D'Artois in the Jim Leslie murder.

However, when McDaniel heard about my radio interview, he was mad. He contacted me on our two-way radio and said, "Bill

Keith, I sent you out there to cover the news, not to make news!"
I didn't grant any more interviews that day.

Caddo Parish deputies Rusty McKinley and B. M. Kitchings
arrived on the scene an hour later to serve as backup to Jones and
Teros, who were still trying to get the commissioner to surrender.[8]
As the hours passed, the crowd was growing so large that McKinley
and Kitchings had to ask the crowd to disperse. At 10:45 A.M.,
several Shreveport police cars arrived on the scene and assisted
the deputies in moving the mass of people away from the area.

"All you folks move your cars and leave the area or we'll call
wreckers and have them towed away," a police officer bellowed
through a bullhorn.

Another officer announced that only members of the news media
would be allowed to remain at the scene. Once the crowd scattered,
police officers placed barricades at both ends of Ashbourne Street
to block wide-eyed sightseers from driving down the street to get a
glimpse of D'Artois.

Throughout the day, King observed the neighbors sitting on their
front porches or watching the spectacle through windows in their
homes. "The waiting went on," she reported. "The sun beat down
on the sidewalk and police officers and newsmen alike jockeyed
for spots in the shade. Some sat on the grass and watched . . . and
waited."[9]

King said later that some of the reporters were eating fried
chicken and hamburgers and drinking Cokes. "The scene under
spreading trees looked like a picnic, not a vigil involving a life-and-
death situation."[10]

John Rasmussen, Shreveport Fire Department chaplain, who
knew D'Artois quite well, asked to be allowed to go into the house
to pray with the commissioner. The officers granted his request.

After Rasmussen departed, D'Artois, wanting to tell his side of
the story, asked Jones and Teros if he could speak with a reporter
from one of the television stations. They told him that before they
would allow an interview, he would have to surrender his weapon.

He refused. The deputies thought he may have wanted to kill himself before the cameras.

Around 1:00 P.M., the commissioner gave fifteen pages of typed material to his wife. Although the contents were not made public, it is believed that, among other things, he had typed a list of the people he had chosen to be his pallbearers in the event of his funeral.

About 2:30 P.M., D'Artois took a shower and asked his family to bring him his dark, pinstriped suit. His wife was allowed to take the suit to him.

By 3:00 P.M., Jones and Teros had been in the midst of the standoff for nearly eight hours, and they had decided to try to apprehend the former commissioner and handcuff him.

"We asked him if he wanted a cup of hot coffee, and when he cracked the door open to take the coffee, we threw our weight against the door and forced our way into the bathroom," recalled Jones.

Jones grabbed D'Artois' gun, and Teros knocked him to the floor and handcuffed him. Teros, a power weightlifter, knew if he could get his hands on D'Artois, he could hold him. "He was grabbing for the gun when we pinned him to the floor," Teros said. "I had him on the floor with his wrists pinned, and he said, 'Oh, my heart,' and we sent for oxygen."

At 3:07 P.M., McKinley came out of the house, yelling, "He's in custody!"[11] Thus, he signaled the end to the eight-hour standoff.

As they brought D'Artois out of the bathroom in handcuffs, his wife and two daughters were crying and holding on to him. Jones remembered the scene as "one of the several emotional outbursts during the ordeal."

The deputies let him spend some time with his wife and family before placing him in a 1977 Chevrolet Impala, an unmarked deputy's car, around 3:21 P.M. He was driven to the Caddo Parish Courthouse, where he was booked on charges of first-degree murder in the death of Jim Leslie.

The waiting was over; the siege had ended.

As I watched the drama play out that afternoon on the sidewalk in front of the D'Artois home, I felt sadness in my heart. Because of the commissioner, I had lived through night flights, getting my family out of Shreveport and away from possible danger; bomb threats at the newspaper; a conspiracy to plant illegal drugs in my car, thus discrediting me as a newsman; and the specter of a hit man from New Orleans in town to kill me. However, seeing the fall of a once-powerful man gave me no satisfaction.

I hope that it's over, I thought. Surely, with D'Artois in custody, the killings and the threats of killing now would end.

And they did end. After D'Artois was arrested, I didn't hear of any further incidents of intimidation or threatening of grand jury witnesses, theft of city funds, air charter flights for personal travel paid for by the city, forgeries of funds allegedly paid to police informants, or funds stolen from evidence envelopes in the police

Shreveport Journal *headline and front-page story of D'Artois' arrest on April 19, 1977.* (Courtesy LSUS Archives—Noel Memorial Library)

evidence room. When the commissioner went to jail, his empire of deceit, dishonor, and death virtually disappeared overnight.

I tried to understand what might have caused the man who was the symbol of law and order in the community to turn against that law and order so quickly and so completely. Lieutenant Merolla, who had worked closely with D'Artois for several years, also thought a lot about the great change in the commissioner's life.

"We thought he may have had a stroke and that affected him," Merolla told me. "Also, he liked to gamble, and his gambling was out of control. Since the commissioner didn't receive a big salary, he had to find a way to feed his gambling habit. But when he was hard up for money, some of the people we knew were gamblers came to see him at his office."

When seeking to understand the rise and fall of George D'Artois, there is an alternative theory to consider.

Lord Acton (1834-1902), the Italian-born historian who became professor of modern history at the University of Cambridge in England, once wrote, "Power corrupts, and absolute power corrupts absolutely."

On one occasion, he told his students, "I exhort you . . . to try others by the final maxim that governs your own lives, and to suffer no man and no cause to escape the undying penalty which history has the power to inflict on others."[11]

I believe the commissioner was obsessed with power. He may have suffered a stroke that crippled some of his mental faculties, but, in my opinion, he was tortured by his own personal demons. There was a blackness, a darkness, and a tempest around his pursuit of power.

"What happened to him is a mystery," Jones told me years later. "George did a lot of good for the police department. I don't know what got him off on the other side." Through the years, he "just kept getting deeper" into the lawlessness that finally destroyed him.

He added, "George was a heck of a nice fellow when he worked with the sheriff's office. Back in 1960 and 1961, he helped out young people when he was off duty, as he would umpire softball and baseball games at the SPAR, Shreveport Parks and Recreation, league."

Ambulance driver Allen McBride, who examined D'Artois after his arrest, said that he looked like he was in "good shape" but had "hyperventilated" and "was pale and real nervous."

The stone-faced commissioner did not speak to anyone when he arrived at the courthouse.

"He showed no emotion or sign of recognition as he passed by perhaps 50 reporters and photographers, whose clicking shutters were the loudest sounds that could be heard as the silent procession moved swiftly down the hall," King wrote in the *Times*.[12]

According to King, "Just as D'Artois reached the point where he would make a right turn to enter the elevators which would take him to the jail, he found himself face to face with newsmen."[13] He did not try to shield his face from the cameras; however, he did lunge at the newsmen and knock down a *Times* photographer. "An instant later the deputies ushered D'Artois into the elevator and the steel door clanged shut."[14]

Caddo deputies once again booked and fingerprinted the former commissioner and Dr. Robert E. Braswell, the parish coroner, gave him a physical examination prior to being extradited to Baton Rouge.

I realized the commissioner probably would not want to live without power and privilege; the charter flights to Arkansas for gambling parties; the praise from the members of the Shreveport business community for keeping law and order; and, yes, the praise from both local newspapers, neither of which heretofore had ever held him accountable for any of his questionable activities. He had enjoyed all those things during his years as commissioner, and the thought of giving them up must have been unbearable for him.

That same day sheriff's deputies arrested another man in connection with the murders of Jim Leslie and Rusty Griffith. They charged Donald D. Gardner, age thirty-nine, of Shreveport, in the deaths of both men.

The last time I saw the commissioner, he had wounded eyes and looked as if he was trapped in someone else's nightmare. There were traces of care and sorrow on his face, with its anemic, wan complexion and lines that radiated from the corners of his eyes. The Baton Rouge deputies led him out of the east entrance of the county jail and put him into the back seat of their unmarked car. He looked in my direction with a dull, vacant expression, like a man who had given the devil a mortgage on his soul. His arrest was the beginning of the end of the mystery that had hypnotized the people of Shreveport for more than a year.

When he saw me standing near the car, he turned his head away and never looked at me again. That afternoon I saw a glimpse of how far some heroes fall.

"D'Artois left the courthouse at 4:40 P.M. in handcuffs and secured by a length of chain attached to a large leather waistband," the *Times* reported. "He was solemn and expressionless as the deputies drove away and headed toward Baton Rouge where he was expected to spend his first night in jail."

Hence climaxed one of the most sensational episodes in the history of the City of Shreveport.

Capital correspondent John Hill had previously been allowed to view the East Baton Rouge Parish jail cell where D'Artois was to be held. Apart from the bars on the windows and the terrazzo floor, Hill noted the cell looked more like a motel room than a jail cell.[15]

The cell was originally built to accommodate overnight stays by out-of-town deputies who were in Baton Rouge to pick up or deliver prisoners. It was separated from the cellblocks that housed more than five hundred other prisoners.[16]

Sheriff Amiss and the prisoner arrived in Baton Rouge at 9:37 P.M. and went directly to the East Baton Rouge jail with sirens blaring and red lights flashing.

"Deputies and Sheriff Al Amiss quickly rushed the haggard looking former Shreveport lawman past news reporters into the booking room where he was booked, fingerprinted and examined by Dr. Louis Mayer, a Baton Rouge surgeon," Ronni Patriquin of the *Journal* reported. The former commissioner did not say anything to reporters or the other sheriff's deputies as he entered the jail.

D'Artois and Gardner appeared before Judge Frank Foil in Nineteenth Judicial District Court in Baton Rouge to hear the formal reading of the charges against them. D'Artois, dressed in standard prison denims with "EBR Jail" printed on the back of his shirt, looked sad and dejected.

"Though D'Artois and Gardner were seated near each other, they did not speak," Hill and Shuler of the *Times* capital bureau reported.[17]

After the hearing, D'Artois and Gardner were taken back to jail, D'Artois to his special cell and Gardner to the regular cellblock area.[18]

Following the arrest, Sheriff Terry answered questions from representatives of the Shreveport news media on why it took his deputies eight hours to apprehend the former commissioner. The sheriff read the following from a prepared statement:

> The situation has been one where the deputies of my department had to make a difficult choice. Mr. D'Artois was armed with a .357 magnum. He was in the confines of his home where there were several persons close at hand, his wife and immediate family as well as his lawyers, friends and our officers.
>
> A forcible arrest with a risk of possible injury [or] to surrender peaceably. I chose the latter route as the better of the two, and I believe the subsequent events have proved my decision to be right. In every such case I consider that human life, or the possible loss of it, must be the major factor in deciding how the matter will be handled.[19]

Once again editorial page editor Jim Montgomery, in another of his powerful and intuitive editorials, placed the story of the arrest of the former commissioner in the proper perspective for our readers and for all the people of Shreveport.

"The bizarre spectacle which put Shreveport into the spotlight again yesterday almost defies acceptance. Such things just don't happen here, in our town; in our own time."[20]

Montgomery pointed out that most of the people in the city and area stood by their radios, waiting for late bulletins on the drama of the former commissioner's standoff with sheriff's deputies. "Bizarre, yes, but then everything about the D'Artois case has been strikingly out of the ordinary. . . . And there is still no conclusion. Mr. D'Artois has not been convicted; he has been arrested. No jury of peers has yet heard a shred of evidence against him in a courtroom. Until he has that full hearing, this bizarre story, stranger indeed, than any fiction, will remain unfinished, and may continue to unfold."[21]

Meanwhile, Mayor Allen, in a complete retreat from reality, said that D'Artois' arrest was no reflection on the city or city officials.

"It's an individual thing. I don't think you could say it's a reflection on City Hall officials, city government or the people of Shreveport."[22] However, he added, "Certainly it's a pity for this sort of thing to happen."[23]

In an interview with Craig Flournoy of the *Shreveport Journal*, Mayor Allen lashed out at the news media, alleging that serving as mayor was like "living in a fishbowl."[24] He also attributed most of the problems to the "nitpicking" harassment by the local news media.

According to the mayor, there had been a rash of resignations by city employees during the D'Artois investigation, and he believed it was brought about by a "continuous harangue over some practices which may or may not be important or significant. It's all been blown out of proportion, but now it's like a growing cancer. I feel the majority of citizens in the City of Shreveport still believe in their city government. You only hear nitpicking complaints from the few who have nothing better to do than to sit around and complain."[25]

What amazed me was after all that had happened—the murder, theft, intimidation of witnesses—the mayor didn't even realize that the lid was off the garbage can.

"I'm just glad it's over and no one was hurt," the newly elected public safety commissioner Terry Hayes said. "Maybe now things can get back to normal."[26]

Perhaps Finance Commissioner Burton's evaluation was close to the truth when he stated, "I think he's probably an ill man," adding that D'Artois' physical health may have had something to do with his recent behavior.

When I read the mayor's statement, I couldn't believe the naiveté of the city's chief administrative officer. Perhaps all the turmoil at city hall and the revelation of graft and corruption in the police department threatened his loss of reason. The tragic life of George D'Artois was not only a reflection on the mayor and the other commissioners at city hall, but it was also a reflection on us all.

For years, the mayor must have heard the rumors of protection and payoffs and rampant gambling in the city, yet he did nothing. He knew that the hundreds of payoff pinball machines were illegal, yet he did nothing. The mayor knew that the several hundred thousands of dollars approved by voters for a new and innovative computerized traffic control system had never been applied to that system and that the money had disappeared and he did nothing. Moreover, he removed Chief Kelley and Chief of Detectives Lanigan and let D'Artois choose the men who were to investigate him.

I personally liked Mayor Allen and believe that though he was weak, he was a good man. Nevertheless, for years, D'Artois had told him what to do, and when the commissioner got into trouble, the mayor didn't have the ability or the courage to run city government.

CHAPTER FIFTEEN

The Affidavit

The warrant issued by Judge Gonzalez for the arrest of D'Artois on a charge of first-degree murder in the death of Jim Leslie was based on an affidavit presented to the judge by Sheriff Amiss of East Baton Rouge Parish.[1]

The affidavit outlined details of the charges against D'Artois. Some of the information had been published previously in our newspaper and presented a sordid tale of evil, deception, and murder.[2] It stated that D'Artois had paid Rusty Griffith (deceased) and Don Gardner the sum of thirty thousand dollars to kill Jim Leslie.

According to the affidavit, on August 5, John Templin, a retired police lieutenant from Shreveport, gave a sworn and notarized statement that on or about Memorial Day of 1976, his wife received a phone call at their residence in Carthage, Texas, from Commissioner D'Artois. Templin said the commissioner asked him to come to room 667 at Schumpert Medical Center in Shreveport to talk to him.

Templin decided to go see his old friend. When he walked into his hospital room, the commissioner put his finger to his lips as though someone else was in the room listening to their conversation.

A few minutes later, police officer T. L. "Bubba" Hardin walked out of the bathroom, shook hands with Templin and left the room. Once the two men were alone, D'Artois reminded Templin they had been friends for a long time and told him there was something he wanted him to do. The commissioner said he could beat all the charges against him if he could "get someone taken care of."

Templin asked, "What do you mean by that—taken care of?"

175

"I need Jim Leslie taken care of, and he is at home alone right now."

Then he informed Templin of Leslie's whereabouts, mentioning that Leslie's family was away from the city at that time. The commissioner wanted him to "find Leslie, put him in his car and do something with him so that his body will never be found."

"I would kill the SOB myself if I could get out of this bed," D'Artois stated.

However, Templin refused to have anything to do with killing Leslie. At that point, D'Artois asked him if he knew anyone who might do the job for him. Templin mentioned the names of Jim Reno and Cliff Guevara, but added, "I don't think either one of them would want the deal."

"Well, just forget the whole thing," the commissioner responded.

Reno, a Shreveport package liquor store operator, later testified in district court in Baton Rouge that D'Artois did ask him to find someone to kill Leslie. According to Reno, the commissioner also invited him to his hospital room at Schumpert. The commissioner offered to pay Reno five thousand dollars to kill Leslie, and he wanted him killed that day.

Reno told the court the commissioner informed him that Leslie lived on South Lakeshore Drive in Shreveport, and he wanted someone to ring his doorbell and "blow him away or to take him out somewhere and bury him so he wouldn't be found." During his testimony, Reno said he turned down D'Artois' offer but acknowledged that the commissioner had previously arrested him on narcotics, burglary, and gambling charges.

Because of his arrests, Reno did not qualify for a liquor license, and D'Artois must have intervened on his behalf, thinking he would ask Reno to repay him by killing Leslie.

On February 28, there was a memorandum filed in Nineteenth Judicial Court in East Baton Rouge Parish by Cliff Guevara. In the memorandum, Guevara stated he too visited the commissioner in the hospital and was asked to dispose of Leslie. Guevara told the commissioner he didn't want anything to do with killing Leslie.

The affidavit noted that about one week after Guevara visited the hospital, the commissioner visited him at his home. Guevara got in the car with him, and D'Artois asked him how much money it would take to get him to kill Jim Leslie. Once again Guevara refused and told the commissioner not to ask him again.

On April 4, 1977, Clayton Kimble stated in the affidavit that he met with Rusty Griffith and Donald Gardner at the Sheraton Inn in Baton Rouge to plan the Leslie murder two weeks before the event. At the meeting, Griffith asked Kimble if he could find someone to kill Leslie for his friend George D'Artois. Griffith emphasized that Leslie had to be killed.

Griffith, Gardner, and Kimble met a second time at the Check Mate Lounge in Baton Rouge, about one week before Leslie was killed. During that meeting, they planned the murder in great detail. Gardner informed the others that D'Artois had someone following Leslie around Shreveport, looking for the right opportunity to kill him. However, the commissioner decided the killing should take place in Baton Rouge, during the heated right-to-work debate, so that organized labor would be blamed for his death.

Gardner and Griffith asked Kimble to kill Leslie and offered him thirty thousand dollars to do the job. Kimble, saying this was not his kind of work, refused. Griffith reminded Kimble of the favors bestowed on him by D'Artois when he was a bar owner and gave him five thousand dollars as an advance for him to hire someone to kill Leslie.

Griffith suggested that Kimble get a man named Bennie O'Quinn to do the killing, but Kimble declined. He thought O'Quinn was too dangerous to have connected with the killing but offered no further explanation on the matter.

About five days before Leslie's murder, Kimble met once again with Griffith and Gardner at the Admiral Benbow Motel on Sherwood Forest Boulevard in Baton Rouge. Unable to hire anyone to do the killing, Kimble returned the money. As a result, Griffith and Gardner decided to kill Leslie themselves, using Kimble as a lookout. But, again, Kimble refused.

Griffith then asked to borrow Kimble's walkie-talkie, which was delivered to him by Kimble a few days before the murder. At that meeting, Gardner and Griffith discussed with him their plan, which was to shoot Leslie as he was getting into his car at the state capitol. However, that plan was abandoned since they thought there would be too many state policemen in the area. Kimble then came up with a simpler plan. He told Gardner and Griffith all they had to do was find out the name of the motel where Leslie was staying and kill him at that location.

The day before the murder, Griffith met Kimble at the Pitt Grill to tell him Leslie was booked at the Prince Murat Inn. The new plan was for Griffith to hide behind the fence in the rear of the inn and wait for Leslie to drive into the parking lot. Gardner would park his car in an empty spot near where Griffith was hiding, and when Leslie drove into the parking lot, he would pull out so Leslie could take his parking space. Then, when Leslie got out of his car, Griffith would shoot him.

Griffith and Gardner delivered a red and white Cadillac to the residence of Steve Simoneaux several days before the killing, according to the affidavit. Kimble drove the automobile from Simoneaux's residence to the Holiday Inn South, where it was delivered to Griffith on the afternoon of July 8. He parked the car next to Griffith's brown Cadillac Eldorado.

The morning after Leslie was murdered, Kimble met with Griffith and Gardner at Denny's. They returned his walkie-talkie to him clear of fingerprints. Gardner relayed the previous night's events to Kimble.

Their plan went off without a hitch, and seconds after the shot was fired, Griffith and Gardner drove away. As they crossed the Mississippi River bridge, Griffith threw the shotgun into the middle of the river, and they returned to Shreveport that night.

Authorities informed the court that the information given by

Kimble was verified by a polygraph examination and PSE administered by Lt. Lee Denison of the Louisiana State Police. He acknowledged the test results showed that Kimble's testimony was truthful.

However, in court testimony years later, Steve Simoneaux, who apparently was present during the murders of both Leslie and Griffith, disputed some of the facts outlined in the affidavit that led to the arrest of Gardner and D'Artois.

Simoneaux, of Simmesport, Louisiana, confirmed in a court hearing in Baton Rouge that he and Clayton Kimble met with Griffith to discuss killing Leslie but that Gardner was not involved.[3] He said that after the meeting, he, Griffith, and Kimble drove around the Prince Murat Inn, where Leslie would be killed, to finalize their plans. Simoneaux further stated that the day following the murder, Kimble told him that after they shot Leslie in the back, the killers drove to Port Allen near Baton Rouge and threw the shotgun in the Mississippi River.

During the court testimony, prosecutor Barton Conradi of the East Baton Rouge Parish District Attorney's Office questioned Simoneaux.

When Simoneaux alleged that Clayton Kimble showed him a "sawed-off shotgun," Conradi asked him what Kimble said about the gun.

Simoneaux said Kimble purchased it for a particular reason.

"What did he say was the reason?" Conradi asked.

"He said it was for a murder he planned to participate in."

"Did he mention the name?"

"Yes."

"What was the name?"

"Jim Leslie."

However, Simoneaux testified in the Griffith murder case that it was Jules Ron Kimbel, whom Griffith believed was his friend, who told him he wanted Griffith killed.

Simoneaux, who passed a lie detector test indicating his testimony was true, later told Anderson of the *Morning Advocate* that he had taken part in both the Leslie and Griffith murders but was not the trigger man.

"Simoneaux said he was some 60 feet away when the [Leslie] killing occurred and that he then drove the killer and two other men from the scene," Anderson reported.[4]

According to Simoneaux, Griffith was not the triggerman in the Leslie slaying and Gardner was not there during the night of the murder. He stated the killer was an unidentified "man from Dallas."

This new piece of information caused me to wonder if Carlos Marcello was involved. I knew that Marcello had connections in Dallas and controlled some of the organized crime there. Did Marcello send a man to kill Leslie to help his friend D'Artois?

Simoneaux said he was also present three months later when the same group killed Griffith and implicated the brothers, Kimble and Kimbel, in the killing. He later testified against them in exchange for a reduced twenty-five-year sentence for armed robbery.

Clayton Kimble also told Baton Rouge sheriff's deputies that D'Artois paid to have Leslie killed. However, his version of events told a different story concerning Rusty Griffith's role.

"Griffith allegedly followed Leslie to the [Prince Murat] motel and told the hit man by walkie-talkie that Leslie was nearing the motel," Anderson quoted Kimble as saying.

So why did they decide to murder Rusty Griffith? According to Kimble, the assassins were afraid Griffith was going to tell authorities what he knew about the Leslie murder as a bargaining chip in his indictment in connection with an international heavy-equipment theft operation. Kimble also said that D'Artois paid the assassins thirty thousand dollars to kill Leslie in an effort to get even with him for testifying against him before a Caddo Parish grand jury.

I have found it quite strange that the suspects in the Leslie and Griffith murders had conflicting testimonies, yet apparently passed lie detector tests.

CHAPTER SIXTEEN

Justice vs. Politics

After the arrest of George D'Artois, the people of Shreveport breathed a sigh of relief as the once great city, brought to its knees by one errant political leader, began the long journey back to a sound justice system.

However, almost immediately East Baton Rouge Parish district attorney Ossie Brown began a feud with Sheriff Al Amiss, a feud that had been brewing for several months and threatened the court case against D'Artois and Gardner. Brown announced on April 26, 1977, he might not offer immunity to certain witnesses whose testimony might be necessary to obtain a conviction against the two men charged in the murder of Leslie.[1]

When reporters reminded him that several months earlier he had said he would be "almost willing to let the triggerman go" if he could convict the man who paid to have Leslie murdered, Brown said he had made the statement "just in talk."[2] It appeared that for some reason Brown had changed his mind and his direction in the prosecution of the case. Asked if he would consider a lesser charge for Gardner, Brown replied, "I just don't know. I'd have to think a long time before I could do that. I don't like to let criminals go."[3]

On Monday, Judge Frank Foil set May 16 as the date for the preliminary hearing in the D'Artois case. At that time, Brown would be required to demonstrate probable cause for why authorities should continue to hold D'Artois and Gardner on the first-degree murder charge.

During a brief appearance before the court that same day, attorney Pat Wilson of Baton Rouge entered the names of Stacey Freeman, William Hall, and Maynard Cush, all of Shreveport, as legal counsel for D'Artois in the proceedings. D'Artois' lawyers entered a motion for a preliminary hearing. They believed there was "no probable cause or valid reason (beyond mere speculation by the East Baton Rouge Parish sheriff)" for holding the former commissioner.

Following the preliminary hearing, District Attorney Brown wasn't sure if he had enough evidence to hold D'Artois. Apparently, Sheriff Amiss's investigators, Lt. Nick Ross and Sgt. Glenn Smith, had not yet given Brown all the evidence they had accumulated. The investigators had turned over some of the evidence requested by Brown, but there was still more to be furnished to the prosecution.

Ross told the *Journal* he believed they had presented sufficient evidence for the preliminary hearing in the affidavit they filed for the arrest warrant for D'Artois. Brown, who announced he would be the chief counsel for the state, admitted to not having "time to evaluate the evidence."[4]

On May 5, Brown opened the preliminary hearing into the Leslie murder by refusing all plea deals.[5] It was apparent to the observers at the hearing that Brown's no-immunity decision jeopardized the state's case against D'Artois and Gardner.

"Right after Brown declared that immunity would not be granted to witnesses Steve Simoneaux, Clayton Kimble and Jules Ron Kimbel, all of Baton Rouge, each of the men took the stand and promptly claimed their rights against self-incrimination refusing to answer all questions," Ronni Patriquin of the *Journal* reported. "Each man even refused to give his full name in response to the prosecution's questions."[6]

When Clayton Kimble was sworn in to testify, Asst. Dist. Atty. John Sinquefield proclaimed, "Anything this man says under oath, we fully intend to use against him."

Bryan Bush, the attorney for Clayton Kimble and Steve Simoneaux reminded the court that his clients had been promised immunity for their testimony. On the other hand, Judge Foil informed Bush that he had heard nothing from the district attorney concerning immunity for the two men and reminded him that the district attorney was the only person who could make such a deal. The judge then advised Kimble of his rights.

Brown told Simoneaux that no immunity was being offered to him for his testimony, and at that point, the witness claimed his Fifth Amendment right to refuse to answer a question.

In addition, the attorney for Jules Ron Kimbel told the court that although his client had not been granted immunity, he would not testify in court without some promise from the district attorney. Kimbel's testimony was critical in order to connect the shotgun killing of Rusty Griffith to the Leslie murder.

"Brown entered the arrest warrants . . . against D'Artois and Gardner into the court record. In the sworn affidavits attached to the warrants, the chief investigators . . . Lt. Nick Ross and Sgt. Glenn Smith, swore that Clayton Kimble and Simoneaux had told them under oath that Griffith had told them that he and Gardner killed Leslie for D'Artois in return for $30,000," Patriquin wrote.[7]

According to investigators, Simoneaux paid the money to Griffith after it had been "laundered" through several accounts with New Iberia National Bank in New Iberia and Fidelity National Bank in Baton Rouge. After Simoneaux, Clayton Kimble, and Jules Ron Kimbel were excused, the prosecution questioned several witnesses who could corroborate certain aspects of what the three men had told investigators.

Investigators Ross and Smith, who were still tying up some loose ends in the case, believed the information in the affidavits for the arrest warrants for D'Artois and Gardner was correct.

"Smith and Ross both testified that they knew they needed more time to investigate when they requested the warrants," Patriquin wrote. "Both law officers said that Sheriff Al Amiss ordered them to get the arrest warrants when they did. Ross said that when he obtained the warrant he did not tell the duty judge, Douglas Gonzales, that he needed more investigation time."[8]

"We felt we had enough probable cause to draw up the warrant, so we did. Evidently the judge felt we did too because he signed it," Ross said.

"Asst. Dist. Atty. John Sinquefield said he and Brown made the decision not to grant immunity to three men whose statements led to D'Artois and Gardner's arrests because the truthfulness of their information could not be ascertained." John Hill reported in the *Times*. "We are not certain they are telling the complete truth about their involvement in Jim Leslie's death. They may be involved to a greater extent."[9]

For this reason, Judge Foil had no choice but to release D'Artois from jail and drop the charges against him and Gardner in the Leslie murder case, announcing there was not sufficient evidence to hold the two men any longer.[10]

"D'Artois left the prison around 7:30 P.M. through a rear gate, away from reporters awaiting his release," Hill reported. "Mrs. D'Artois and their two daughters, who had been with him at the prison, left separately from the front entrance in a family automobile. Their destination was not known. In issuing his ruling, Judge Foil made it clear that D'Artois and Gardner can be charged again with Leslie's death if new evidence is developed linking to the crime."[11]

Judge Foil issued the ruling after two days of hearings during which the district attorney presented all the evidence developed by sheriff's investigators. The judge also pointed to inaccuracies in the sheriff's affidavit that led to the men's arrests.

Gardner, named in the arrest warrants as an accomplice in the Leslie murder, was turned over to Sheriff Schiele of Concordia Parish. He still faced charges in the October murder of Rusty Griffith, his former business partner. D'Artois, who also had charges pending for stealing city funds, was scheduled for trial on June 13.

Meanwhile, in an unusual twist in the Leslie murder case, District Attorney Brown announced another break in the case might be near.

"He indicated that he believes that the three state's witnesses who refused to testify against D'Artois and Gardner . . . are actually more involved in the case than they led sheriff's deputies to believe," Ronni Patriquin of the *Journal* reported. "He said that his office has independent information linking Steve Simoneaux, Clayton Kimble and Jules Ron Kimbel . . . to the murder."[12]

According to the district attorney, a state police polygraph operator said that although Simoneaux and the brothers were telling the truth in their statements to investigators, the test indicated they were holding back important information.

In another bizarre twist, D'Artois' attorneys planned to file a lawsuit against Sheriff Amiss for either false arrest or the violation of civil rights.

"There is no question we are preparing a suit," Maynard Cush, one of D'Atrois' attorneys, told the Associated Press, adding the nature of the suit had not been determined. "We could go into federal court under the Civil Rights Act against Amiss personally, and we have a possible tort action [civil damage] in state court."[13]

When asked about the possibility of a lawsuit being filed against him by D'Artois, Amiss said he really didn't care.

The *Times'* capital correspondent John Hill attended the hearings in Judge Foil's court and made the following comments:

> Had it not been a gravely serious matter, the George D'Artois hearing in district court here last week would have been high comedy. . . . Playing the part of the Keystone Kops would have been the sheriff's department, which obviously had no evidence backing up the first-degree murder charges against D'Artois and Shreveporter Donald Gardner. . . . By the time of the hearing . . . almost everyone knew what the outcome would be. The sheriff's office simply did not have a case.[14]

During the hearing, a rumor began to spread claiming the Baton Rouge Police Department, the known nemesis of Sheriff Amiss and his department, had a legitimate eyewitness to the Leslie slaying.

"Gary James, a BRPD intelligence officer subpoenaed to testify by Gardner's attorneys, said his office has a verified eyewitness who has named those present when Leslie was killed," reported Hill.

"James' testimony was terminated when he said Donald Gardner was not among the persons named by the witness."

In another development, Concordia Parish authorities released Gardner from jail and dropped all charges against him in the Griffith murder.

After returning to his home in Shreveport, D'Artois' heart condition continued to deteriorate. His attorneys announced he might have heart surgery in the immediate future to replace a valve.

On May 23, D'Artois filed a $4.5 million lawsuit in federal court against Sheriff Amiss. The suit claimed that D'Artois was "humiliated and falsely imprisoned" when he was arrested for the murder of Jim Leslie.[15]

"The federal court suit filed Monday asks $2 million in punitive damages from Amiss and $500,000 each for humiliation, loss of reputation, false imprisonment, malicious persecution and libel," J. L. Wilson of the *Times* reported. "In addition to Amiss, the petition also lists other unnamed officers as defendants."

The suit alleged that Sheriff Amiss and his investigators should have known that there was insufficient evidence to ask for an arrest warrant for the former commissioner and "that one or more alleged facts" sworn to in the affidavit "were in fact untrue and were not of sufficient character to justify any belief therein."

Wilson continued by writing, "The petition charged that the officers' accusations 'were calculated and done in such a manner, not for the purpose of serving justice and the needs of the people, but for the purpose, among others, of gaining publicity, and furthering the individual ends of one or more of the defendants before the public eyes.'"

The suit also charged "one or more of the defendants" with assembling members of the news media at D'Artois' home "in anticipation of requesting that a warrant be served in front of . . . news media." When the arresting officers arrived at D'Artois' home he went "in a state of panic, did barricade himself in a room in the house, from which he was only convinced to leave some hours later. As a result of the arrest, D'Artois was subjected to 'any number of days of incarceration, damaging your plaintiff's character, subjecting him to ridicule and harassment, and damaging complainant's already impaired health," Wilson stated.

D'Artois' attorneys requested a trial by jury on the issue of damages but by a judge on all other matters in the suit.

Sheriff Amiss, when informed of the suit against him, noted that D'Artois had been fighting for months to stay out of court on charges of felony theft.

"If he can't stand trial on criminal charges in Shreveport, how can he go to civil court?" Amiss asked. "I sure would like to talk to him under oath," Amiss said, noting that the investigation into the murder of Jim Leslie is continuing.

CHAPTER SEVENTEEN

The Last Roll Call

After the judge ordered his release from jail, D'Artois returned home to Shreveport. However, it soon became apparent to everyone that he was a very sick man. On June 7, his attorneys called a news conference. According to Bill Hall, one of his several attorneys, recent tests revealed D'Artois had three blocked arteries, one of which was one hundred percent obstructed and two others more than ninety percent blocked. The former commissioner would undergo triple-bypass heart surgery at St. Luke's Hospital in Houston the next morning.[1]

The next day, the *Journal* reported that the former commissioner's condition was so critical after the surgery on Wednesday that the surgeons had to operate again that night.[2] D'Artois, whose heart was beating with "artificial help," was recovering in ICU, surrounded by his family. According to family members, D'Artois never regained consciousness after the surgery.

His surgeon, Dr. Grady Halliman, revealed that sections of arteries from D'Artois' leg were transplanted to the heart area "to serve as bypasses for two blocked arteries in front of the heart and one on the side." On Friday, two days after his surgery, D'Arois' doctors announced they were using an intraaortic balloon pump to help the heart pump blood.

However, D'Artois died at 9:15 A.M. on Saturday in St. Luke's Hospital.

The family announced services were to take place at First United Methodist Church, where he was a member. The Reverend Dr. D. L. Dykes, pastor, and the Reverend Jim Moore, associate pastor, would officiate. He would be buried in Forest Park Cemetery under the direction of Osborn Funeral Home. Survivors included his wife, Billie Claire Best D'Artois; one son, George Wendell Jr.; and two daughters, Mary Cecile and Elaine Claire, all of Shreveport; and a brother, W. F. D'Artois of Garland, Texas.

The *Journal* reflected on the former commissioner and his career in an editorial that more than likely represented the feelings of most of the people of Shreveport.

> The book is closed on George Wendell D'Artois. There will be no more chapters of a career that took an incredible, tragic twist in the end.
>
> Death bore out his insistence that he was a very sick man. Not even the miracle techniques of Houston's heart specialists could save him.
>
> Left behind is the enigma of the man. Why did his life collapse in grand jury indictments and murder charges? Why did he capture nationwide attention by holding off arresting officers with a gun?
>
> Had he lived, perhaps the enigma could have been resolved. At least, he would have had his day in court. Death denied him that, even as it released him from further pain.
>
> It should be remembered that four times the voters of Shreveport elected George D'Artois to public office. Four times they had faith enough to entrust him with the management of their public safety department.
>
> In return, he gave the city improvements in the department's services and helped build facilities that were badly needed. Those positive aspects don't mitigate the negative aspects of his tenure in office, but they do help paint a more complete picture of the man.
>
> The events of George D'Artois' last year of life are still too fresh to permit objective assessment. Emotions in this community still run too high. But for now, there is sincere sympathy for his family and friends.[3]

There are a number of theories on why Commissioner George D'Artois fell from grace.

Dist. Atty. Lynne Abraham of Philadelphia, Pennsylvania, once said, "When the police are indistinguishable from the bad guys, then society has a serious problem."

We experienced that very problem in Shreveport. Most of us who lived through the D'Artois saga—when he was riding the whirlwind—repeatedly asked the question: What happened to George D'Artois?

Here was a man highly respected in the community and throughout Louisiana. He had worked with young people while serving with the Caddo Parish Sheriff's Office. He had easily won reelection to office three times. He was married to a beautiful woman and had three good-looking, intelligent children. He lived in Spring Lake, one of the most fashionable neighborhoods in the city. He drove a Cadillac and served as the czar of law and order over several hundred police officers and firefighters who loved and respected him.

Again, I ask the question, what happened to him that would cause him to risk everything?

Captain Burns thinks his heart condition may have affected his behavior. Lieutenant Merolla believed the commissioner may have had a series of strokes, of which the public was unaware, and the strokes could have caused him to go over the edge.

Some believe that over a period of time he became seriously addicted to gambling and did not have the desire or the willpower to give it up. And, as he lost more and more money gambling, he had to find new and creative ways to fund his habit.

I personally believe that the commissioner was obsessed with power. He was unquestionably the most powerful man in Shreveport and even told the mayor how to run the city. The thought of losing that power, for any reason or under any circumstances, was not an option in his personal or political life.

Howard Bronson, the publisher of the *Times* during the D'Artois era, told me years later, "People in politics sometimes let people's adulation affect them in different ways. I think George felt like he could get away with anything. He felt like he could be imaginative for a lot more than the salary he was making."

Perhaps it was the graven image he had of himself, something strange and mysterious that no one could identify or comprehend, that ultimately led to his downfall. Although there are many unanswered questions concerning Commissioner D'Artois, there is one unavoidable principle that governs all life: death clears up everything, and there's no promise of a happy ending.

CHAPTER EIGHTEEN

The D'Artois Day in Court

Almost two years after the former commissioner's death, his attorneys made public the thirteen-page statement he typed as Caddo Parish sheriff's deputies tried to arrest him at his home in April of 1977.[1] The letter, a rambling defense of all charges against him, was addressed to his wife. He told her that he was "completely innocent" of all charges against him in the murder of Jim Leslie.

"In the letter he also denied any knowledge of the misappropriation of city funds while serving as Shreveport's public safety commissioner," Susan Parker reported in the *Journal*.[2]

He alleged that he was the victim of efforts to discredit him by the Caddo Parish district attorney, the *Times,* and East Baton Rouge Parish sheriff Al Amiss.

"This is the most stupid thing I have ever heard of in my life," D'Artois wrote. "But this goes to show you what a stupid sheriff like Amiss and a small two-bit sheriff can do."[3]

D'Artois' attorneys planned to introduce the thirteen-page document into evidence in a $5.5 million false-arrest suit against Amiss and two of his detectives, Nick Ross and Glenn Smith. The lawsuit, filed on behalf of D'Artois' widow and his children, was scheduled to begin on January 15, 1979, before Judge Tom Stagg in federal court in Shreveport. The original suit against Amiss was for $4.5 million.

In the letter, D'Artois also claimed that the editor and publisher of the *Times* pressured District Attorney Richardson into bringing charges against him.

"D'Artois wrote that he knew nothing about 'the Jim Leslie case' and hardly knew Rusty Griffith, who was believed to have had knowledge of the Leslie murder," Parker reported. "I had nothing to do with either men. I had no money to pay anyone . . . I know nothing about anyone who did."[4]

The commissioner said his constitutional rights had been violated when Sheriff Amiss leaked stories to the news media prior to his arrest at his home on Ashbourne Street. He also asserted that District Attorney Richardson did "the dirty work for *The Times*." "I wonder the price?" he asked.

The commissioner told his wife not to forget "the four flushers at City Hall" should she decide to press legal action on his behalf. He listed the so-called "four flushers" by name: Mayor Calhoun Allen; attorney John Gallagher; his assistant, Neckley Ferris, and any "others who sold me down the river. I hope that you will find some lawyers that are not afraid to sue these people because I know you will win."[5]

The letter also contained instructions to Billie Claire regarding the couple's "property on St. Vincent, his VA benefits, bank accounts, and some of his outstanding bills," Parker reported. "He then assured his wife and three children of his 'love' for them, adding, 'I just cannot take this punishment anymore.'"[6]

As he closed the thirteen-page letter, he gave Billie Claire a list of the men he wanted to serve as his pallbearers in the event of his death. They included Stan Lewis, a local businessman; Johnny Bright, a labor leader; P. D. Leon, a former city jailer; and attorneys Pat Looney and Stacey Freeman, who later filed the suit for the D'Artois family. He also instructed his wife to ask the Reverend Dr. Dykes, who had preached at Jim Leslie's funeral, to deliver the funeral sermon.

The D'Artois family and attorneys representing Sheriff Amiss's insurance company reached a dramatic settlement in federal court in January of 1979.

"Terms of the settlement were not made known and apparently will not, according to principals in the case," Thomas Mitchell and James Burns reported in the *Journal*. "At 10 minutes to noon a note was handed the judge and the jury was excused. In less than half an hour the judge returned to announce the settlement. . . . According to *Journal* sources, the D'Artois family was offered an unknown sum of money on Wednesday to settle the suit but family members rejected the offer."[7]

"I'm glad it's over with," the former commissioner's widow said as she left the courtroom.[8] They had agreed on another offer.

Throughout the final trial, the D'Artois family was waving sadly at a parade that had long since passed them by.

The absurdity of it all was what amazed me. The out-of-court settlement between the D'Artois family and Sheriff Amiss left so many questions unanswered.

The public's patience was sorely tried when the two parties began private negotiations in the middle of a trial, making the settlement, and then refusing to give the details of that settlement. It just seemed incongruous to me that a settlement made during the course of a trial could be kept secret.

The public had been exposed to the trial for a week. To be left hanging seemed unfair to me. And, because of the heavy backload of cases, the court really didn't need this kind of useless waste of its time.

As I thought about the settlement, it dawned on me there were other ramifications. Will we ever know if Sheriff Amiss acted with reckless abandon, as the D'Artois family attorneys charged? The preponderance of evidence pointed to the commissioner as the man who ordered the murder of Jim Leslie. However, there were still some nagging questions in my mind: Why did he do it? Was it to keep Leslie from testifying against him in his trial on charges of attempted felony theft? Or was it for vengeance?

I had hoped that the answer to some of these questions might emerge from the trial. None did.

On the surface, it appeared the D'Artois family and their attorneys won a great victory and Sheriff Amiss suffered a great defeat.

I heard that the sheriff was fuming because his insurance company had not consulted him before they settled with the

D'Artois attorneys, and some observers believed that Amiss had the case won. However, representatives from his insurance company knew there would be appeals and those appeals would cost the company a lot of money. Hence, they decided to settle and end the whole ordeal. Of course, the attorneys for the insurance company also faced the possibility that the jury would decide on behalf of the plaintiffs.

I guess what troubled me most was that the trial was a logical platform for prior undisclosed information on the Leslie murder to come to light. There were people who believed that Sheriff Amiss was correct when he identified Griffith as the man who pulled the trigger that killed Leslie. Nevertheless, due to the lack of cooperation among the various law enforcement agencies in Baton Rouge, the name of that man probably will never be made public.

Did D'Artois carry the secrets of the Leslie and Griffith murders with him to the grave? We will never know.

Epilogue

The George D'Artois story was front-page news for more than a year in our newspaper and in every other major newspaper in Louisiana. Even though that was thirty years ago, ghosts of the past still haunt the once-proud city of Shreveport. Time is unforgiving, and the scars are still there, surfacing as wounds on the history of a city that temporarily lost its way and was brought to its knees by the worst scandal in its long history. Like all great cities with great people, Shreveport recovered and today is one of the finest cities in the South.

I believe *The Commissioner* is an important story that bears retelling, even thirty years later. Perhaps we learned a great lesson from the life and times of Commissioner George D'Artois, and I hope we will never have to learn that lesson again.

During the course of writing this book, I became more and more convinced that vigilance is the price we pay for freedom and a free press is fundamental to a free society made up of people who are essentially good but, at times, poisoned by evil.

Spanish-born American philosopher, essayist, and poet George Santayana warned us that those who fail to learn the lessons of history are doomed to repeat it. I've wondered what we can learn from remembering those terrible days of deceit, dishonor, and death.

One lesson, I think, is that as a society we must resolve to hold public officials accountable for their wrongdoing while in office and do our very best to find candidates who are honest and trustworthy to run for public office. We must remember that life is to be lived forward, never backward and that faith and fear both deal only with the future.

In 1977, the *Times* received the Freedom of Information Award from the Louisiana Press Association for exposing Commissioner D'Artois the previous year. Although the award was presented to the newspaper, it named the four members of the enterprise team, Charlotte Burrows, Orland Dodson, Margaret Martin, and Lynn Stewart; editorial writer Jim Montgomery, and myself.

Fred Bacon, speaking on behalf of the association at the awards ceremony, said, "This is an award which is not sought. . . . Rather, it is an award, which is thrust upon a newspaper. A situation is created by others to which it must react. How it reacts to this situation will determine whether or not it is worthy of the recognition that goes with this award."

Bacon stated the winner of the Freedom of Information Award must demonstrate the following three qualities to a high degree:

> First, he must have the intelligence to recognize that the freedom of information principle was being violated. That an effort was being made to deny information to the public. The public, I might add, which he is responsible for keeping informed.
>
> Second, he must have the courage to act to prevent the violation in spite of threats or reprisals.
>
> Third, he must have the professional competence to thoroughly investigate, to research, to document, and to print the full and complete facts and the persistence to stay with the story to the very end.

That same year McDaniel received a letter from the Pulitzer committee notifying him that our newspaper was a finalist for the coveted Pulitzer Prize gold medal for public service for its investigation into D'Artois.

"Now that the Pulitzers have been announced, as chairman of the Public Service Jury, I can tell you that your entry was among the finalists in our consideration," wrote Norman A. Cherness, chairman of the Public Service Jury for the Pulitzer Committee. "I know that 'almost' isn't enough, but I thought you and your staff might like to know that your entry was among the very most impressive."

We finished second to our East Texas neighbor, the *Lufkin News*. Jim Montgomery summed up our thoughts best when he wrote in an editorial,

> Except for a good-humored mutter about being 'almost,' we'll just say that if we couldn't win the Pulitzer this year, we're glad our Lufkin colleagues did. Their stories dealt with a Lufkin youth who died of brain damage received in U.S. Marine Corps training camp and led eventually to reforms of Marine recruiting programs. But here again, they won the award because they refused to accept 'official explanations' when they knew something was wrong and the public had a right to know about it.

During the writing of this book, I tried to locate some of the main characters in the D'Artois drama. I found a number of them and renewed contact with a lot of old acquaintances. These men and women were such an integral part of the story, and they were all heroes. Several of them have achieved great honor in the journalism profession. Others have retired and live with their memories of the anguish and hope of the late 1970s. Some have passed away.

Editor Ray McDaniel retired from the newspaper in 1985 and died in 1991 while on a deer hunting trip to West Texas. He was as tough as nails and at times could be quite severe, but I loved and respected the courageous editor.

The *Times* publisher Howard Bronson moved to Mobile, Alabama, on the shores of the Gulf of Mexico, where he serves as the publisher of the *Mobile Register*. Bronson told me in a telephone interview that he loves living in Mobile and serving as publisher of the *Register*, a newspaper that has had a significant circulation increase in recent years when most newspapers are in decline.

Charlotte Burrows, assistant managing editor and a member of the enterprise team, retired and lives in Shreveport, where she is involved in various church and community activities.

Margaret Martin, another enterprise team member, is still writing for the *Times*. She has worked there for more than thirty years.

Orland Dodson, the gifted enterprise team writer, died in 1987.

Lynn Stewart, the enterprise team editor, served for a number of years as director of communications for Louisiana State University in Shreveport. She held the same position with Centenary College of Louisiana until she retired in 2007.

After a distinguished career as editorial page editor of the *Shreveport Times*, Jim Montgomery joined the *Journal* and continued writing editorials that, through the years, received national acclaim and awards. In 1994, he was one of five finalists for the Pulitzer in editorial writing.

John Hill retired from the *Times* capital bureau in Baton Rouge after thirty-four years.

Marsha Shuler now works for the *Baton Rouge Morning Advocate*. She has had a very successful career covering Louisiana legislature for that newspaper.

Allan Lazarus, managing editor for the *Times,* retired in 1991 after forty-six years and remains in Shreveport.

City editor Will McNutt retired and lives in Shreveport. In 2006, at the age of eighty-five, he took a tour of historic castles in England.

My former partner Elaine King works for Louisiana State University Medical School in Shreveport in the institutional public relations department as a lobbyist.

J. L. Wilson is an entrepreneur and businessman living in Port Allen, Louisiana.

Journal editor Stanley Tiner is editor of the *Sun Herald* in Biloxi, Mississippi, and won the 2006 Pulitzer Prize for public service for the newspaper's coverage of Hurricane Katrina.

Baton Rouge Morning Advocate reporter Bob Anderson, who wrote the chilling story of the murder of Rusty Griffith, still works for the newspaper. He serves as the bureau chief for the Florida Parishes.

Allan Stonecipher, the erudite *Journal* columnist, lives and works in Florida.

Mayor Calhoun Allen died several years after the D'Artois scandal.

Commissioner George Burton retired and is enjoying his well-deserved retirement in Shreveport. In 2006, I met him and his wife at a Shreveport restaurant. While we were reminiscing about our former days at city hall, I apologized for being so rough on him and everyone else during the investigation. He smiled and said, "You were just doing your job."

I also located several of the heroic police officers who took a stand for justice even when it could have cost them their lives or the lives of their families.

When I began my research for this book, four of the so-called "Dirty Five" were still living:

Chief Kelley died Sept. 10, 2006, five months after my last interview with him, at the age of ninety-one. Right up to the end, he continued to drive his car and do investigative work for clients. He lost his wife, Hazel, in 2005 after sixty-seven years of marriage.

Captain Sam Burns retired as an assistant chief. His wife Patti died in 2006. He lives on Cross Lake and tries to keep up with all of his old police buddies.

Chief Kenneth Lanigan, the tough Irish cop and my friend, also lost his spouse, Jo Ann, in 2006 and is trying to work his way through his terrible loss. I hope he will find new meaning and purpose to life in the days ahead.

Lt. Robert Merolla, who retired as an assistant chief, lives on a country estate with his wife, Bobbi, in Bethany, Louisiana, not far from Shreveport. Merolla, who has those Italian good looks, doesn't look much older today than he did thirty years ago.

Major James Byrd, head of the Division of Special Investigations, has passed on.

The commissioner called them the "Dirty Five," but I like to remember them as Shreveport's "Untouchables."

Caddo deputy J. W. Jones, one of the men who arrested D'Artois at his home, retired and lives in Shreveport.

His partner, Bob Teros, retired after twenty-four years as a deputy sheriff. Upon his retirement, he became the chief of security for a large pharmaceutical company in Shreveport, where he lives with his wife.

Carolyn Leslie, Jim's Leslie's widow, in a phone conversation, stated the family is doing well. She also reflected on the tragic loss of her husband: "It was a very sad time. I'll never forget it."

Their son, Scott Leslie, lives in Shreveport and works as a bellman for the Horseshoe Casino.

A short time after D'Artois' death, Captain Burns wrote a letter to McDaniel. He said if the *Times* had not taken a stand against political corruption in the city, within a few short months organized crime would have moved into Shreveport.

Thanking them, Captain Burns wrote, "The Police Department and the people of Shreveport are in your debt for what you have done."

APPENDIX A

The Legacy

What is it about Louisiana politics that could produce a man like Commissioner George D'Artois and dozens of other politicians who are either going to jail, in jail, or out of jail?

The answer is to be found in the terrible legacy that former governor and senator Huey P. Long left for the politicians who followed him. His legacy is alive and well in Louisiana to this very day. Herewith, we explore that legacy.

During Huey Long's tempestuous reign as the Louisiana "King-fish," he ruled over a state that some called a "banana republic." Even after his death, his scandalous influence infected politics and political stargazers in the state for the next half-century.

After Long traveled to Washington as a United States senator, he was succeeded as governor by his longtime friend Oscar Kelly "O. K." Allen. They had been friends since their early days together in Winnfield, Louisiana. Allen was a state senator from the Winnfield area and served as Long's legislative floor leader in the senate for several years. Since Long knew he could trust Allen, he handpicked him to be his successor, and from 1932 to 1936, Allen was a "puppet" governor whose strings were pulled by Long.

Allen actually called his term in office the Long-Allen administration. Long controlled the state from Washington, D.C. with a daily telephone call to Allen.[1] As in Long's administration, there were countless irregularities during Allen's term in office. For instance, on two occasions, he pardoned New Orleans crime boss Carlos Marcello, and some believe he received payoffs in exchange for the pardons.

Allen suffered a cerebral hemorrhage in 1936 as his term in

office was ending. Richard Leche, a New Orleans attorney, was elected governor that same year. Huey Long's younger brother Earl was elected lieutenant governor.

Huey Long once prophesied that the men who followed him in the governor's office would get into a lot of trouble without him there to watch out for them. That prophecy was fulfilled in the Leche administration.

Leche believed a politician who is poor is a poor politician. "When I took the oath of office, I didn't take any vow of poverty," he told a group of friends right after his inauguration. His declaration set the stage for a continuing cycle of lawlessness in the state. In fact, the year 1939 was known as the beginning of the era of the "Louisiana Scandals."

According to the *Gambit Weekly,* an award-winning New Orleans newspaper, some 150 people, including Governor Leche and James Smith, the president of Louisiana State University, were indicted on charges such as income tax evasion; misuse of WPA labor, a federal program that provided jobs and income to the unemployed during the Great Depression; material theft; mail fraud; kickbacks; and conspiracy. Leche resigned from office in the midst of the scandal. Smith lost $500,000 of state money speculating on the stock market. He skipped out to Canada with another $500,000 but later came back to Louisiana to stand trial. Leche and Smith both received prison sentences.

After serving only five years of a ten-year sentence, Leche was pardoned by Pres. Harry Truman; even today, the pardon is cloaked in mystery. Why would President Truman take such an active interest in a little-known former Louisiana governor?

Upon his release from prison, Leche practiced law in New Orleans and served as a lobbyist. Back then, there was little or no shame among politicians who ran afoul of the law.

When Leche went to prison, Lt. Gov. Earl Long, who became known throughout the state as "Uncle Earl," served as governor for one year. In 1948, he was elected to a full four-year term. The younger Long had the smug egotism and fiery conviction of a former nobody. He followed in the footsteps of his brother and tried to centralize absolute power in the state. He encouraged the state legislature to abolish the Civil Service System to increase patronage in the governor's office.[2]

Long continued many of the programs initiated by his brother, such as free lunches for schoolchildren, a vocational school system throughout the state, and he encouraged the legislature to pass a law that made the salaries for black and white schoolteachers the same. He continued bridge and highway construction programs and assistance to the elderly.[3]

In the 1952 election, he was defeated by reform candidate Robert Kennon, primarily because of the fallout from the "Louisiana Scandals"; however, he was elected again in 1956 as Louisiana proved to be a political graveyard for reformers.

During his last term in office, Long carried on a running battle with the segregationist state senator William "Willie" Rainach. Rainach wanted to purge the lists of registered voters to remove the names of all black voters and maintain strict segregation in response to the United States Supreme Court decision that declared "separate but equal" schools unconstitutional.

During a debate on the floor of the senate, Long shouted to Rainach, "A lot of people are following you, not because they agree with you but because they're scared of you!" Long, who realized that the black people in the state were some of his strongest supporters, opposed Rainach's evil scheme. To his eternal credit, he was a champion of blacks and the poor and saved their right to vote.

Long also became something of a spectacle and public embarrassment during those days. In a televised speech, he hurled obscenities at the legislators, according to *American Heritage* magazine. The magazine reported he started chain smoking and carried a soda-pop bottle filled with grape juice and gin around with him everywhere he went.

A. J. Liebling, Long's biographer, once said, "In Earl's speeches, his thoughts chased one another on and off the stage like characters in a Shakespearean battle scene."[4]

Eventually, it became obvious to everyone, including his family members, that he had become incoherent and out of control. However, they did not know if it was from his heavy drinking or some kind of mental illness.

American Heritage reported his wife Blanche, after consulting with Huey Long's son Russell, arranged for a Louisiana National Guard plane to fly her husband to a mental institution in Galveston, Texas, where she had him committed.

Blanche later told a reporter from *Life* magazine,

> They say that when Earl gets out of the hospital he will take his certificate of health and take it out on the campaign trail with him. Then he can say he is the only man in the race who is sane. The people will laugh and be happy again because they know he is the only man in the state who really knows their wants and needs. And I'll be happy again, too. I will know in my heart of hearts that he is well again. I've lived with this twenty-seven years and I love him very much.

Long wasn't nearly as crazy as everyone thought he was. He managed to be released from the hospital in Galveston, but when he arrived back in Baton Rouge, Blanche had him committed again, this time in the Louisiana State Hospital for the Insane in Mandeville. The wily Long used his power as governor to fire the hospital administrator and replaced him with an administrator who released him. After his release, Leibling noted, "He departed on a long tour of recuperation at out-of-state Western racetracks."

It was also during his last term in office that he met a New Orleans stripper by the name of Blaze Starr and carried on a torrid, and very public, romance with her for years. At this time, his mojo was working, and he was strokin' his rabbit's foot in order to stay in tune with the people of Louisiana. The movie *Blaze*, starring Paul Newman as Long and Lolita Davidovich as Starr, told the story of their chance meeting in a New Orleans nightclub and the scandalous affair that followed.

Blaze Starr once wrote in her journal: "When I met Earl, he seemed to be an average crazy old man." As they spent more time together, she fell in love with him and stated her dream was to marry him and "live happily ever after."

"I can't wait until the day he leaves Blanche to marry me," she wrote. "I know she will find out and be furious that a stripper . . . is taking a husband away from a high-class woman like her."

Long continued the affair with Starr until he died in 1960, just one week after being elected to the United States House of Representatives. They never married.

Edwin Washington Edwards was the most popular governor ever to enter the political arena in Louisiana and the first French-Catholic governor of the state in the twentieth century. Edwards, though far more sophisticated, also followed in the legacy of Huey Long.

Edwards was born in rural Avoyelles Parish to a poor family of tenant farmers known as sharecroppers. A brilliant student, he graduated with honors from Louisiana State University in Baton Rouge, and he earned a law degree from the same institution when he was only twenty-one. After graduation, he moved to Crowley, in the heart of Cajun country, and began practicing law.

The populace elected him to four full terms, which is more than any governor in Louisiana history. His Cajun political style and ability to speak fluent French even eclipsed the political career of the roguish Long.

Edwards known by most as the "Cajun Fox" was a smooth-talking, silver-haired ladies' man. Some people called him "Fast Eddie" for he had a sharp political mind and liked to make a fast buck, even if he had to do it outside the law.

I first met Governor Edwards in 1975 when Will McNutt, my city editor at the *Shreveport Times,* asked me to cover the governor's speech at Avenue Baptist Church in the black community. I rather enjoyed his speech, which at times sounded more like a sermon, with its strong political overtones laced with passages from the Bible.

The members of the church talked back to the governor as he spoke saying, "Amen, Governor," "Come on, now," "That's alright, Governor," and "My Lord, my Lord!" After the service ended, the church members served lunch in the fellowship hall where he was their honored guest.

During the lunch, I had the opportunity to interview him for my story and found him to be a likeable, charming, charismatic political leader. Through the years, I heard him speak several more times and wrote other articles about him. I was always intrigued at his keen intellect and vast knowledge of the intricacies of state government.

Most of us who lived through the Edwards years heard the rumors that he was taking payoffs for gubernatorial favors. However, because of the heritage of graft and corruption in the state, most people only whispered about the rumors and paid little attention to his womanizing and gambling.

The governor was also popular with other religious groups in the state including members of the United Pentecostal Church. Edwards' knowledge of the Scriptures and charismatic appeal led the Pentecostals, undoubtedly the largest group of straight-and-narrow Christians in the state, to invite him to their annual convocation in Tioga, Louisiana, attended by as many as fifteen thousand people.

During one of his speeches to the Pentecostals, Edwards said, "I have been accused of drinking, gambling and womanizing but I want you to know that I don't drink and two out of three ain't bad."

There was a thunderous applause, and it was apparent that day that they loved their governor, even with his shadowy reputation. I believe the members of the church supported him during all four of his gubernatorial campaigns.

In 1964, Edwards was elected to the Louisiana State Senate and then to the United States House of Representatives. In the election of 1971-1972, with strong support from the Cajuns, Creoles, and blacks in the state, he was elected governor of Louisiana. Organized labor unions in the state also strongly supported him.

With this win, Edwards began four corruption-plagued terms as governor. He dominated politics in the state, both in and out of office, for the next twenty-five years. Throughout his checkered career, his theme was taken from a French saying: *"Laissez les bons temps rouler,"* or "let the good times roll." They rolled on for nearly a quarter-century during which Edwards garnered the reputation of being a high-stakes gambler and a crafty politician. During his first administration, some in the state criticized him for his frequent trips to Las Vegas, where he became a well-known celebrity gambler.

One Thanksgiving season the *Times* received a United Press International (UPI) wire story, saying Edwards had lost fifty thousand dollars over the weekend. When reporters asked him about his Thanksgiving trip to Las Vegas and his gambling, he became indignant and said it was none of their business.

"Print it just like that: None of your d*** business," he said.

He confirmed he and his wife traveled at the expense of Harrah's and that a jet from the casino picked them up in Baton Rouge. Asked if he took guests with him, he replied, "That is also none of your d*** business," according to UPI. "I have no comment to make on the story. It was my family holiday and I enjoyed it."

His second term in the governor's office was marked by scandal when it came to light that his wife Elaine, in 1971 or 1972, had received ten thousand dollars in cash from Tong-sun Park, an agent of the Korean government, during the so-called "Koreagate" scandal that also reached into the halls of Congress. In addition to the ten thousand, Park gave the Edwards a very expensive pearl-inlaid coffee table, which they proudly displayed in the governor's mansion.

The FBI questioned Edwards about the gift from Park, and he appeared before a committee in the U. S. House of Representatives looking into "Koreagate." However, it was never clear exactly what Edwards did, if anything, for the money, and no charges were ever filed against him. It is known that the Koreans purchased 100 million tons of rice from Louisiana planters from 1966 to 1976.

The *Shreveport Journal* commented on the Edwards-Park connection in an editorial on November 4, 1976:

> So far, it has not been proved that Park had any official connection with the South Korean government, and it may be that Edwards did not technically violate any laws. But the whole affair had a bad odor. Giving large amounts of cash to a member of the governor's family just doesn't leave a nice taste in the mouths of most Louisianans.

After "Koreagate," Edwards was the subject of several other investigations by the United States Department of Justice. His intellect made him hard to catch and even harder to convict. For instance:

In 1979, the FBI investigated Edwards to determine if he was involved in the Bribery/Labor scandal. Carlos Marcello and Charles Roemer II, Edwards' commissioner of administration, were convicted of bribery in the scandal and went to prison. The Fifth United States Circuit Court of Appeals later overturned both of their convictions. Edwards was not indicted.

In 1980, during his third term in office, the Justice Department investigated Edwards for his part in a suspicious scheme to provide a tax shelter for state employees. However, the grand jury did not indict him. When his four-year term ended that year, he was appointed to serve temporarily on the Louisiana Supreme Court.

In 1985, the Cable News Network (CNN) reported that he was indicted and went to trial for taking payoffs relating to state hospital and nursing home permits. Edwards said the $2 million he made from the deal was legal. Although the prosecutors believed they had a strong case against him, the jury failed to convict.

In 1998, a federal grand jury indicted Edwards and his son Stephen for extorting millions of dollars from various individuals seeking riverboat gambling licenses in Louisiana.

While working at the *Shreveport Journal* I spoke with a family that told me a bizarre story about the Edwards administration. Their son was serving time in Angola, and an official in Governor Edwards' office had contacted them through a second party. They were told that for $2,500 the state parole board, appointed by the governor, would grant their son a parole.

The family said they didn't have the money and would not have given it to the governor even if they had it. They spoke of how unfair that brand of Louisiana justice was and asked me to investigate the matter to see if something could be done to stop the kind of illegal activity that rewarded prisoners from wealthy families and punished those from poor ones.

Obviously, when I began my inquiry into the matter, no one in state government would talk to me about it. After all, who would admit that the governor of the state was taking payoffs for pardons and paroles.

Ironically, Nolan Edwards, the governor's brother, was shot and killed by a man who had received a pardon from his brother. There was never any evidence of the assailant having paid the governor for his pardon.

Edwards' only political defeat in his long and colorful career was in 1987 when he made his first attempt at an unprecedented fourth term in office. During a televised forum, a reporter asked the other candidates, "If you fail to make the runoff, will you support Edwards?" Several of them skirted around the question, but Charles "Buddy" Roemer III replied, "No, we've got to slay the dragon. I would endorse anyone but Edwards."

That statement in that forum gave the Roemer campaign a boost in the polls—from last place to first—and in the days and weeks following, most of the major newspapers in the state endorsed him. Meanwhile, Roemer printed thousands of "Slay the Dragon" bumper stickers that appeared on automobiles all throughout the state.

Roemer won the election.

During his four years in office, Roemer alienated just about everyone in the state including his wife who left him soon after the election. He made all the Democrats in the state mad when he switched from the Democratic Party to the Republican. He angered most Republicans when he vetoed a strong antiabortion bill that had passed overwhelmingly in both the Louisiana Senate and the House of Representatives.

In 1991, Edwards decided to make another run for the governor's office and that election was one of the most unusual in Louisiana history, as Edwards attempted to make a political comeback. Edwards, who had recently been charged with taking payoffs from hospital developers in the state during his previous administration, soon became the frontrunner in the race. He ran on a platform that promised to open Louisiana to a state lottery and riverboat gambling

The third man in the race was David Duke, a member of the Louisiana House of Representatives from Jefferson Parish and a former wizard of the Ku Klux Klan. He claimed he had renounced all his ties to the Klan and was a born-again Christian.

Both Edwards and Roemer knew that Duke was a formidable candidate. In 1989, he had run against Sen. J. Bennett Johnston of Louisiana. Johnston won the race, but Duke received sixty percent of the white vote in the state. As the governor's race progressed, it was evident that Duke had a lot of grassroots support from many of the antigambling, anti-Edwards groups and from a large number of Christians who really believed, or at least wanted to believe, that Duke had experienced a religious conversion and was no longer a white supremacist or Klan sympathizer.

Edwards' supporters distributed bumper stickers that read: "VOTE FOR THE CROOK: It's Important." Edwards won the primary, and Duke finished second, ninety thousand votes ahead of the incumbent Governor Roemer.

The runoff between Edwards and Duke was a slugfest, and the two of them spent so much money that some referred to the race as the "Second Louisiana Purchase." Duke hammered away at Edwards for his alleged wrongdoing and the numerous federal investigations during his previous three terms as governor. He also came out in opposition to organized gambling, affirmative action, and hiring quotas in the state and that resonated with a lot of people, particularly those in North Louisiana.

Meanwhile, Edwards and his campaign gurus found old films of Duke wearing a Nazi uniform and saluting the German flag with a "Heil Hitler" and used excerpts of the films in television ads. The images of Duke as a Nazi sympathizer and pictures of him in his white robe at a Klan rally were too much for most Louisianans.

Edwards received endorsements from former Republican governors David Treen and Roemer, and Republican president George H. W. Bush also said he favored Edwards over Duke. So once again, the people turned to Edwards who was elected by a wide margin.

After his election, Edwards said that he wanted to leave a good legacy. That caused some to believe and hope that the corruption of the previous three administrations was behind him. Little did we know that the worst was yet to come.

Edwards kept his word on the issue of gambling, pushing bills through the Louisiana legislature that opened up the state to virtually every form of gambling.

Author Tyler Bridges wrote a very provocative book entitled *Bad Bet on the Bayou: The Rise of Gambling in Louisiana and the Fall of Governor Edwin Edwards.*[5] He said that fast money, dirty politics, and systematic corruption have been the hallmark of Louisiana politics both before and after the Edwards administrations.

"Louisiana is our most exotic state. It is religious and roguish, a place populated by Cajuns, Creoles, Christian conservatives, [and] Rednecks. . . . It is a state that loves good food, good music and good times," an editorial review of the book pointed out.[6]

According to Bridges, during the past thirty years, Louisiana has seen "a parade of elected officials convicted of crimes."

The list includes a governor; an attorney general; an elections commissioner; an agriculture commissioner; three successive insurance commissioners; a congressman; a federal judge; a state senate president; six other state legislators and a host of appointed officials; local sheriffs; city councilmen; and parish police jurors.

In the 1990s, Bridges stated, Louisiana "plunged headlong into organized gambling authorizing more games of chance than any other state." Governor Edwards, who for years had engaged in high-stakes gambling in Las Vegas, led the charge on behalf of casino gambling and used his "razor-sharp mind and catlike reflexes to stay one step ahead of the law."[7]

In 1999, Edwards once again was indicted, along with Jim Brown, state insurance commissioner, and others in the case of the Cascade Insurance Company. He was acquitted, but Brown went to prison.

Nevertheless, in 2000, his luck ran out. He and his son Stephen were convicted on seventeen of thirty-four felony counts of racketeering in the riverboat gambling license case. CNN reported that during the four-month trial, prosecutors "presented hundreds of hours of wiretaps and videotape of witnesses who told of payoffs left in dumpsters and money strewn about the floor of Edwards' million-dollar home, even hidden under ducts in the freezer."

"The verdict marks the first victory in three attempts by the government to convict four-time Louisiana Governor Edwin Edwards of corruption," reported CNN correspondent Charles Zewe. "Four years ago he was acquitted of racketeering after two trials."

When Edwards heard that he could be sentenced to as many as three hundred years in prison, he smiled and said, "I don't think I'll be able to serve the time."

Edwards' extortion trial in the riverboat license scandal was a high-profile trial that became a national news story. During the trial, Edward J. DeBartolo, who at the time was the owner of the San Francisco 49ers, admitted to investigators that he paid Edwards several hundred thousand dollars to help him secure a very lucrative riverboat license.

After Edwards' conviction, the *Las Vegas Sun* reported that Players International, one of the organizations accused of payoffs to Edwards, voluntarily agreed to withdraw from Louisiana and pay a fine of $10.2 million.

Edwards once boasted, "They have not made a prosecutor who could ambush me," but apparently he had never heard of Eddie Jordan, the attorney who prosecuted him in the riverboat licensing scandal.

"I think that we have to begin a process of removing the stain of corruption from Louisiana, and I think that, in this case, we have confronted corruption squarely in the face and we have dealt with it appropriately and fairly," Jordan told CNN.

"In 40 years of public life, Edwards developed a reputation as a quick-witted wheeler-dealer, an unabashed gambler, womanizer and populist champion of the underprivileged, despite being investigated two dozen times," said CNN correspondent Zewe.[8]

After his conviction, Edwards said he might return to public life after his stint in prison. He referred to a newspaper poll that showed fifty-three percent of the respondents would vote for him again should he seek an unprecedented fifth term as governor.[9]

"I may give them a chance," he said.

When asked what he thought prison life would be like, the silver-haired Edwards joked, "It'll probably be captivating. I will be a model prisoner as I have been a model citizen." [10]

Two years after he entered prison, he filed for divorce from his wife, the former Candy Picou, whom he had married in 1994 when she was twenty-nine and he was sixty-seven. He said she had "suffered enough" through the trial and his imprisonment.

Reflecting on his long and turbulent career, he said, "I feel comfortable with my place in history."[11]

Edwards is serving a ten-year prison term in a federal penitentiary in Oakdale, Louisiana. He is scheduled to be released in 2011. In 2005, Candy was arrested for threatening a police officer. David Duke is also serving a prison sentence for mail and income-tax fraud.

My good friend Michael O'Keefe, former state senate president from New Orleans, was also convicted and went to prison. I knew O'Keefe and voted for him as senate president on a couple of occasions. He had a wonderful wife and two handsome children. He was always there to help freshman senators like me.

When the citizens of Louisiana elected Governor Dave Treen to office, O'Keefe, a Democrat, became the second most powerful man in the state. He served eighteen months in the federal prison in Seagoville, Texas, in the mid-1980s for swindling $900,000 from his business partners in an apartment complex project.

Then, in 1999, he began serving a nineteen-and-one-half-year sentence for illegally taking millions of dollars from a failed insurance company. I still can't imagine how a nice guy like Michael O'Keefe ended up in prison or what caused him to get into trouble in the first place.

After he went to prison the first time, I sent him several inspirational books that I thought might give him some hope for the future and forgiveness for the past. After all these years of investigative reporting, I've never felt anything but sadness when a great man like Michael O'Keefe goes down in shame and dishonor.

APPENDIX B

The Legacy Continues—
Crooks and Other Scoundrels

Several months after we closed the books on the D'Artois investigation, Stanley Tiner, the editor of the *Journal,* offered me the job of city editor of the afternoon newspaper. In this new position, I would supervise ten reporters and be responsible for all the local news coverage in Shreveport.

Since it was quite a promotion and included a rather substantial salary increase, I said goodbye to all my friends at the *Times* and moved across the hall to the *Journal.* However, before I accepted the position, I insisted I be allowed to continue investigative reporting. Tiner enthusiastically endorsed the idea.

He also granted permission for me to join the investigative reporters and editors organization, made up of representatives from newspapers throughout the United States and Canada who have a basic interest in that journalistic pursuit. I attended two of their national meetings in Denver, Colorado, and Boston, Massachusetts, where I became acquainted with some of the finest investigative reporters in the nation, men and women from the *Los Angeles Times,* the *Philadelphia Inquirer,* the *Chicago Sun Times, Newsday,* and a host of other newspapers.

I worked on several major stories during the *Journal* years and believed that investigative reporting was my forte. During those years, I saw first hand that the corrupting influence and legacy of Huey Long was alive and well in nearly every area of state government and in certain municipalities. There were certainly enough scandals to keep me busy.

At the *Times,* I had been involved in two major investigations, including the George D'Artois and the Public Utilities Department scandals. I had also taught a class on investigative reporting at

Louisiana State University in Shreveport. After a few successful investigations, I developed a reputation as a man who could be trusted.

One of the most important things for an investigative reporter to
remember is never to betray his confidential sources; otherwise he
will develop a reputation as a reporter who cannot be trusted. Also,
the reporter must display a determination to follow through on a
story and not back away from sensitive situations of wrongdoing
in local or state government even when the going gets rough as it
usually does.

One day that determination nearly cost me my job as city editor.
There was a young man who worked for me at the *Journal* by the
name of Craig Fluornoy, who, in my opinion, was one of the best
reporters ever to hit the city.

As I was working the city desk one day, he asked me if I would
go with him to the little town of Cotton Valley east of Shreveport in
Webster Parish to help him with what he thought could turn out to
be a very sensitive interview.

He had been working on a story believed to involve payoffs to
an assistant district attorney for reducing criminal charges from
felonies to misdemeanors and wanted me to go with him to interview
a man who reportedly had made such a payoff. Obviously, the
importance of such a story centered on the fact that misdemeanors
carry far less fines and/or jail time than felonies, and it would be to
the criminal's best interests to have the charges reduced.

We drove my Chevrolet Vega to Cotton Valley and went to the
home of the man in question. I had always tried to teach the
young reporters like Flournoy to "break the ice" so to speak before
beginning the interview. For instance, I told them to talk about the
weather, inquire about children and grandchildren, or a beautiful
picture on the wall.

However, when Flournoy and I walked into the man's home,
Flournoy got right in the man's face, asking, "Did you pay that
assistant district attorney to lower the charges against you for your
arrest?"

Flournoy talked very fast and had a way of spitting out a light spray of saliva when he talked, and there he was, in the man's face, spitting and trying to get him to confess that he had paid off a public official.

The man turned to his wife and said, "Get me my shotgun, I'm going to kill both of these sons of b******."

I looked around the room to find something to hit the man with, but all I could find was a table lamp. I had decided that I wasn't going to let him kill Flournoy and me over a newspaper story. Rather, I would hit him with that lamp if his wife returned with the shotgun. She exercised good judgment and did not bring the shotgun. I saw we were getting nowhere with him, so I suggested that we return to Shreveport.

However, I knew I had to tell Tiner about the incident. It was later in the afternoon when I arrived at his home in Blanchard, north of Shreveport, and told him what had happened. Tiner's face turned red, and he said, "Keith, I ought to fire both of you for doing a fool thing like that. You and Flournoy ought to have more sense than to get yourselves killed."

He was so mad I just kept my mouth shut. He eventually cooled down and ordered me never to do anything like that again.

"You don't have to worry about me, boss, I've learned my lesson," I replied.

I had always tried to follow two principles in my reporting: first, there is no story worth getting hurt over and, two, there's no story worth getting a confidential source in trouble. I knew I had violated the first principle that afternoon in Webster Parish.

By way of a footnote, Flournoy left the *Journal* and went to work for the *Dallas Morning News,* where he and his partner, George Rodrigue, received a Pulitzer Prize in journalism in 1986 for the investigation of subsidized housing. They uncovered patterns of racial discrimination in public housing not only in East Texas, but all across the United States. Their articles brought about significant reforms.

Throughout the next few months, I received several calls from people in various areas of the state who related stories of political abuse and wrongdoing to me. One of those involved Agriculture Commissioner Gil Dozier of Louisiana.

Dozier was a man's man, over six feet tall, with heavy brows, hair shot with gray, and a network of fine lines gathered at the contours of his eyes. He was a fine-looking, clean-cut kind of guy.

I heard him speak at a civic club in Shreveport, and I was impressed with his intelligence and his commanding presence. I believed he had all the skills and attributes to become the finest agriculture commissioner in the history of the state. That success could have catapulted him into the governor's office.

Dozier was also a daredevil and exhibited a cavalier attitude toward life. For instance, he would go to Mexico and participate in a game that was illegal in the United States.

In this game, the Mexicans would dig a deep pit and put Dozier down in it armed with a shotgun. A jaguar would be dropped into the pit. At that point, it became a game of man versus beast.

Crowds stood around taking bets on whether Dozier or the big cat would win. Dozier always seemed to win.

One day, I received a call from a man with agriculture interests in Homer in Northeast Louisiana. He accused Dozier of using his office to coerce people into giving him money in order for them to receive agriculture-related licenses for various business enterprises.

Ronni Patriquin, of the *Journal* capital bureau, worked with me on the story and interviewed State Rep. Loy Weaver of Homer, a former FBI agent. Weaver had firsthand information on some of Dozier's illegal methods. He said Dozier even tried to force people dealing with his office to give him business stock in their companies in return for political favors.

Predictably, when Patriquin spoke with Dozier, he called Weaver's charges "a bold-faced lie" and said Weaver had political motives for trying to discredit him. However, when Representative Weaver testified before a Livestock Charter Commission, he gave details of Dozier's attempts to solicit funds or stock from persons connected with livestock auction barns in the state.[1]

Weaver explained to the commissioners that all auction barns in the state must be licensed by a certain commission appointed by Dozier, one in which Dozier served as chairman.

"Weaver said the agriculture commissioner actually accepted money from Floyd Giles of Homer, a former employee of the Homer Livestock Commission, promising Giles a license to establish a livestock auction barn to compete with the one owned by his former employer," Patriquin and I reported.

Dozier denied the allegation and asserted he'd "never received any money from Mr. Floyd Giles."

I called Giles at his home in Homer, and he confirmed Weaver's allegation of the payoff for a political favor. He said he paid the money to Dozier with the understanding that he would receive a charter for a new livestock barn.

"I gave that man [Dozier] a contribution, and I was supposed to get a charter, and so far I haven't gotten anything, not even a conversation," he told me. "That man has promised me everything in the world, and now he won't even talk to me."

Giles also provided me with the time and place they met and confirmed there were witnesses who saw him give the cash to Dozier.

Representative Weaver told Patriquin that Giles didn't consider the money a contribution to Dozier's reelection campaign. He made it very clear he was giving him the money so that he would help him get the charter for the new auction barn.

During the course of our investigation, Patriquin and I learned that on another occasion Dozier offered a state agriculture loan to an auction barn owner in Lake Charles, Louisiana, to help rebuild the barn that had burned. Dozier allegedly sent a representative to the owner, saying the loan would be approved if he gave him stock in his company. However, the owner refused, and the loan was never granted.

With the above evidence in hand, and other witnesses from throughout the state who claimed Dozier tried to extort money from them, a Baton Rouge grand jury indicted him on several charges, including racketeering, bribery, and extortion. He was convicted and sentenced to eighteen years in prison.

Ironically, his predecessor Dave Pierce was tried and convicted of similar charges when he was in his seventies. However, because of his age, he served no time in prison, according to Capitol Watch, a guide to Louisiana State Government.

Ronni Patriquin and I believed that our investigative stories on Dozier helped rid the state of one more political pariah who used his office for personal financial gain.

However, after serving only four years of his sentence in a federal penitentiary, he was given a presidential pardon by Pres. Ronald Reagan. We never understood why.

A good investigative reporter survives on the "tips" from men and women who know the difference between right and wrong and have a passion for ethical standards, whether in business, education, or government.

Once, I received an intriguing tip from an anonymous caller who worked for the Caddo Parish School Board. I was told about a so-called "brain-wave analyzer" invented by Dr. John Ertl of Toronto, Canada. By some misfortune, the "analyzer" made its way down to Louisiana and into Caddo Parish schools.

According to Dr. Ertl, the device used several electrodes attached to a student's head to test for learning deficiencies, brain damage, or emotional problems. The test, or as Dr. Ertl called it "the application," took about five minutes per student.

Representatives of Neural Evaluation, Inc. of Shreveport apparently had a contract with Dr. Ertl and administered the tests to 4,500 students in the Shreveport area.

The anonymous caller stated the program cost the parish $270,000, and once the tests were completed, none of the results were ever evaluated. The caller who believed the testing was a rip-off of taxpayers' money, said that even if the testing were of value, school authorities would never know for sure since there was no evaluation of any of the students tested.

I learned the first request to the Louisiana Department of Education for funding came from Clydie Mitchell, special education director for Caddo Parish schools. Mitchell made a special trip to

Baton Rouge to sell the state education officials on the concept of the brain-wave analyzer. That was three months before Neural Evaluation, Inc. was incorporated in Louisiana.

During my investigation, I learned that Dr. Tom Clausen, director of the state's Special Education Division, made the final decision to fund the unorthodox child-testing method.

Several Caddo Parish school-board members told me they had heard of the program but knew very little about it. Most of them were shocked to learn that none of the students' tests had been evaluated, even though the tests cost $270,000.

Mitchell told me the state picked the Caddo Parish schools for the research program because state officials believed the Shreveport area would be ideal for the pilot program. She did not tell me why.

A few days after I wrote the original story, I learned that Mitchell was on the payroll of Neural Evaluation, Inc., and the company had paid her six thousand dollars for her work on behalf of the company while she was still an employee of the school board. It was a clear conflict of interest, but no one seemed to care.

Her contract with the company was discontinued after she appeared before a federal grand jury in connection with a probe of the company.

I also interviewed Doyan Foster, president of Neural Evaluation, Inc.: "They [state officials] selected Caddo Parish because she [Mitchell] had one of the best special education programs in the state."

However, a spokesman for the Department of Education in Baton Rouge contradicted Foster's claim. He said it was Mitchell "who came in and made a formal presentation" on the brain-wave analyzer and convinced the education officials to try the program.

The first phase of the testing involved some fifteen hundred students and the second phase three thousand. State education officials recommended that the last three thousand to be tested should be preschool children and already-identified special-education students.

After my stories appeared in the *Journal,* and all the brouhaha surrounding the futuristic brain testing settled down, the school board ordered Superintendent Walter Lee to prepare a report on the testing and Mitchell's involvement with the company administering the tests.

In the midst of my investigation, Kelly Nix, state superintendent of education, stopped all payments to Neural Evaluation, Inc. He said he took the action after a panel of psychologists and other experts in the brain-wave testing field from throughout America were unable to determine the validity of the program.

A footnote to the hocus-pocus brain-wave testing program:

Through the years, I made friends with a couple of FBI agents who worked in the federal building in Shreveport, and we often shared information.

Billy Thomas, a veteran agent, told me that my investigation had saved the people of Louisiana a lot of money and embarrassment. Thomas said that one of the agents from Shreveport was in the office of Commissioner of Administration Charles Roemer in Baton Rouge seeking some information on an FBI investigation. When Roemer was away from his desk, the agent saw a proposed contract on his desk and briefly glanced at it.

The contract was between the State of Louisiana and Neural Evaluation, Inc. to test schoolchildren in every parish in the state with the brain-wave analyzer. There are sixty-four parishes in the state. If each school board throughout the state tested the same number of students as in Caddo Parish, that program would have cost the taxpayers of Louisiana $17.2 million for testing some 288,000 students.

Only in Louisiana!

"Nothing is ever dull in Louisiana politics—three insurance commissioners, three convictions, three prison terms. Can Bayou Staters endure more excitement, or is the nightmare finally over?"[2]

It has to be more than coincidence that three of the previous commissioners of insurance in Louisiana served prison terms for malfeasance in office:

Sherman Bernard served forty-one months in a federal prison in Alabama in the mid-1990s after he was found guilty of taking bribes disguised as campaign contributions. Bernard was imprisoned in the Federal Prison Camp in Montgomery, Alabama. There he was a member of the work detail and rode a bus to a large auditorium in the city, where he changed light bulbs and swept floors. He told friends he had a good view of the state capitol from his room in the prison.

Doug Green is serving a twenty-five-year sentence for his role in the Champion Insurance scandal. He took $2 million in illegal campaign contributions from various insurance companies doing business in Louisiana.

Jim Brown served six months in the federal facility in Oakdale, Louisiana, after being convicted for lying to an FBI agent. He was indicted on fifty-six counts of conspiracy, mail and wire fraud, false statements, and witness tampering. However, he was acquitted on forty-three of those charges.

Gambit Weekly pointed out in its "Commentary" section:

> Stories about the historic corruption and mismanagement of Louisiana's Insurance Department have become so commonplace that nothing surprises voters anymore. To list every indiscretion would take more space than is available in this newspaper. But let us hit the dark highlights, which illustrate the tragedy of bad governance—and ultimately the erosion of the faith of the people in a democracy.[3]

The newspaper pointed out that Bernard was a very popular commissioner who was elected to four terms in office.

> Bernard was followed immediately by another miscreant—Doug Green. . . . The young insurance commissioner, who looked like the boy next door, took $2 million in illegal campaign contributions from Champion Insurance Co., a Baton Rouge insurer that was tossing and turning in a financial mess but was kept alive by Green.[4]

When Champion went out of business, the company owed $150

million in unpaid claims. Guess who eventually paid those claims. Right, the taxpayers in the state.

Jim Brown became the commissioner after Green went to jail.

I knew Brown and had followed his career, from state senator to secretary of state to his unsuccessful campaign for governor. He was a genuinely nice person. I liked him and worked with him some during my years in the Louisiana Senate. Brown was a country boy from rural Louisiana, and when he went south, he met up with a bunch of professional high rollers, and they rolled him.

"He was convicted . . . of lying to the FBI, which was exploring alleged back-door deals for a failed insurance company when it caught the commissioner in several misstatements," the *Gambit* reported.

I don't know why he lied to the FBI on thirteen different occasions about Cascade Insurance Company. It was a bad decision and ruined him politically. After his conviction, other stories of graft were uncovered in his office.

The legislative auditor found a pattern of payroll fraud in the department. Several of Brown's employees "were paid for hours they did not work and were reimbursed for expenses they did not incur," according to the *Gambit*. The story shed light on several other aspects of the case.

> The auditor provided names, including Fess Irvin, a former LSU basketball player. . . . Also named was Richard Chambers, who allegedly filed 209 false expense reimbursement forms and was paid $11,247 for travel mileage to which he was not entitled. . . . Brown's deputy commissioner of management and finance approved those and other questionable expenses— including those incurred by employees who were on leisure trips, working out at the gym and performing in a play.

Huey Long would have been proud of that crowd!

"After Mardi Gras, the streets are messy, revelers are weary, and everyone's got a hangover," Shari Dwyer wrote in *Leader's Edge* magazine. "That could describe the condition of the Louisiana insurance business after the political orgy that ended with three successive insurance commissioners serving jail time."

In her article entitled "Easy Money," Dwyer asks the question: "What is it about Louisiana, anyway?"

She explained that the state has a distinctive foreign flavor, with roots in France and Spain. It also has three separate cultures: "the Cajuns in the rural south; the more cosmopolitan Creoles in the cosmopolitan New Orleans area, and Baptists in the state's northern region."[5]

Perhaps John Hill, the veteran *Times* capital correspondent, summed it up best when he wrote in the *Baton Rouge Business Report*: "Anywhere you put people and other people's money in the same room, you've got to watch out."

Although in her article Dwyer gave us some deep insight into the political corruption among the insurance commissioners, I must add that it is all a part of the Huey P. Long legacy, a legacy that just won't go away.

Then there is the incredible story of "Dollar Bill."

It's always been a mystery to me why some intelligent men make such foolish mistakes. Congressman William Jefferson of New Orleans is a good example of that troubling mystery.

I've known Jefferson since 1980 when we served together in the Louisiana Senate. He was a graduate of Harvard Law School, had a beautiful wife and family, and an infectious smile. To know him was to like him

While serving in the Louisiana Senate, Jefferson made two unsuccessful runs for mayor of New Orleans. In 1991, he was elected to the United States House of Representatives. He represented most of the greater New Orleans area. His election was a great victory for him and the black communities he represented since he was the first black man elected to Congress from Louisiana since Reconstruction.

In 2006, FBI agents raided his homes in New Orleans and

northeast Washington. News reports claimed the agents had found ninety thousand dollars in marked bills wrapped in aluminum foil and hidden in frozen-food containers.

His congressional office was also raided; it is believed to be the first such raid in history. Although the FBI agents did not disclose why they wanted to search his office, Fox News reported that it was in conjunction with a public corruption investigation in which two of Jefferson's former associates had made guilty pleas.

The raid created quite a firestorm as members of the House of Representatives said it violated the separation of powers principle in the Fourth Amendment. However, a federal judge ruled that the FBI raid was legal.

Jefferson, aware that the high-profile investigation was causing some concern back home in New Orleans, invited the news media to the federal building in that city to hear his official statements.

He told reporters and others that he was innocent of all charges and would not resign from his post during the investigation even though two of his former associates had implicated him in a bribery scheme.

Jefferson, referring to his former associates, said they had been his friends but caved in to enormous pressure from FBI agents.

"In order to protect themselves, they have now characterized their relationship with me, or with my family, in ways that fit neatly within the government's mistaken legal theories," he said, according to the Associated Press.

Former Jefferson aide Brett Pfeffer admitted to bribery-related charges and testified that Jefferson demanded money for his help with two telecommunications projects being set up in Africa, particularly in Nigeria and Ghana. He said Jefferson wanted five to seven percent ownership of the companies.

"Vernon Jackson, chief executive of iGate Inc., a Louisville, Ky., telecommunications firm, subsequently pleaded guilty to bribery, admitting he paid hundreds of thousands of dollars to Jefferson and his family members in exchange for the congressman's help obtaining business deals in Nigeria, Ghana and Cameroon," the AP reported."[6]

The AP also reported that Jackson's plea bargain with the

Justice Department required him to cooperate with the FBI in the ongoing investigation of Jefferson. The total amount of the bribes is believed to be between $400,000 and $1 million, according to court documents in the proceedings against Jackson.

The FBI videotaped Jefferson receiving $100,000, in one-hundred-dollar bills, in a leather briefcase at the Ritz-Carlton hotel in Arlington, Virginia.

According to Allan Lengel and Jonathan Weisman of the *Washington Post,* Jefferson reportedly told Lori Mody, an investor who was wearing a wire for the FBI, that it would be necessary for him to give Nigerian vice president Atiku Abubakar $500,000 to guarantee contracts for Mody's company.

"As court records, sworn affidavits, plea agreements and search warrants attest, it was quite a deal, one of several involving at least seven business entities, nearly a dozen family members and hundreds of thousands of dollars sloshing through bank accounts, all to Jefferson's personal benefit," Lengel and Weisman reported.[7]

Jefferson's money-making schemes involved his wife Andrea, two brothers, five daughters, and two sons-in-law.

"As a member of the House Ways and Means trade subcommittee, Jefferson has traveled repeatedly to Nigeria and other Western African countries and met with their leaders," Lengel and Weisman reported.[8]

Political observers in New Orleans believed the allegations of widespread corruption surrounding Jefferson fit into a pattern of personal financial controversies he has faced all of his life.

"He broke with his mentor Ernest 'Dutch' Morial, New Orleans' first black mayor, in the late 1970s over a steep bill Jefferson delivered for legal work that Morial had assumed was free," Lengel and Weisman reported.

Allan Kurtz, an independent New Orleans political consultant, said, "That's why we call him 'Dollar Bill.'"

Although we believe in a presumption of innocence, and would hope that all these allegations against Jefferson are untrue, the evidence continues to pile up.

After reading a number of stories about the Jefferson investigation, I'm amazed at how prolific he has been in his money-making schemes, and I wonder how he ever had time to represent the people in his district.

In December of 2008, Jefferson lost his bid for a tenth term in Congress to Republican Ahn "Joseph" Cao, a Vietnamese immigrant. Jefferson was scheduled to stand trial in early 2009 on sixteen counts of bribery, conspiracy, and racketeering.

Notes

Chapter One

1. Associated Press, "Labor Strife Figure Murdered," *Shreveport Journal,* 13 May 1977, sec. A, p.1.

2. Ibid.

3. Ken Grissom, "Murderer Lurked Near Only Empty Parking Space," *Shreveport Journal,* 12 July 1976, sec. D, p. 12.

4. Ibid.

5. Ibid.

6. Ibid.

7. Ibid.

8. *Times* Capital Bureau, "Bussie Issues Statement in Leslie Slaying," *Shreveport Times,* 10 July 1976, sec. A, p. 5.

9. Marsha Shuler, "Holstead Leads House in Prayer for Jim Leslie," *Shreveport Times,* 10 July 1976, sec. A, p. 5.

10. Ibid.

11. Ibid.

12. *Times* Capital Bureau, "Steimel Makes Statement on Leslie Murder," *Shreveport Times,* 10 July 1976, sec. A, p. 5.

13. Ibid.

Chapter Two

1. Sam Burns, interview by author, Shreveport, Louisiana, 20 March 2006.

2. "Funeral Held for Jim Leslie," *Shreveport Journal,* 12 July 1976, sec. A, p. 1.

3. Ibid.

4. Stanley Tiner, "Jim Leslie: The Best and the Brightest," *Shreveport Journal,* 10 July 1976, sec. A, p. 2.

Chapter Three

1. Enterprise Team, "D'Artois Tried to Use City Funds to Pay Personal Bill," *Shreveport Times,* 15 May 1976, sec. A, p. 1.

2. Ibid.

3. Ibid.

4. Ibid.

5. Ibid.

6. Ibid.

7. T. P. Kelley, interview by author, Shreveport, Louisiana, 11 April 2006.

8. Wanda Warner, "D'Artois in Hospital, Denies Misuse Try," *Shreveport Journal,* 15 May 1976, sec. A, p. 1.

9. Ibid.

10. Jim Montgomery, "Commissioner D'Artois Should be Relieved of Duties," *Shreveport Times,* 16 May 1976, sec. B, p. 2.

11. Ibid.

12. Ibid.

13. Ibid.

14. Lynn Stewart, "Preferential Treatment Confirmed by Records," *Shreveport Times,* 15 May 1976, sec. D, p. 1.

15. Ibid.

16. Ibid.

17. Ibid.

18. Margaret Martin, "D'Artois Is Figure in Race Track Suit," *Shreveport Times,* 16 May 1976, sec. A, p. 1.

19. Ibid.

20. Ibid.

21. Ibid.

22. Ibid.

23. Burns, interview.

Chapter Four

1. Kelley, interview.

2. Burns, interview.

3. Kelley, interview.

4. Ibid.

5. Burns, interview.

6. Charlotte Burrows, interview by author, Shreveport, Louisiana, 28 June 2006.

7. Burns, interview.

8. Kelley, interview.

9. Burns, interview.

10. Kelley, interview.

11. Burns, interview.

Chapter Five

1. Lynn Stewart, interview by author, Shreveport, Louisiana, 1 August 2006.

2. Howard Bronson, interview by author, Mobile, Alabama, 1 August 2006.

3. Charlotte Burrows, Margaret Martin, and Lynn Stewart, "Misuse of City Funds Found by *Times* Survey," *Shreveport Times,* 25 April 1976, sec. A, p. 1.

4. Ibid.

5. Ibid.

6. Ibid.

7. Ibid.

8. Burns, interview.

9. Burns, interview.

10. Bill Keith, "D'Artois Defends Accounting," *Shreveport Times,* 27 April 1976, sec. A, p. 1.

11. Ibid.

12. Ibid.

13. Marsha Shuler and Bill Keith, "We Will Fight Back," *Shreveport Times,* 4 April 1976, sec. A, p. 1.

14. Ibid.

15. Orland Dodson, Margaret Martin, and Lynn Stewart, "Allen, D'Artois Travel Records Not Itemized," *Shreveport Times,* 5 May 1976, sec. A, p. 1.

16. Carl Liberto, interview by author, Shreveport, Louisiana, 11 April, 2006.

17. Marcia Desmond, "Southern Research Asked to Probe Use of City Funds," *Shreveport Journal,* 5 May 1976, sec. D, p. 1.

18. Jim Montgomery, "Audit Critical Areas," *Shreveport Times,* 6 May 1976, sec. A, p. 6.

Chapter Six

1. "The Books Are Closed," *Shreveport Journal,* 13 June 1977, sec. A, p. 4.

2. Craig Fluornoy, "The Incident at Little Union Church," *Shreveport Journal,* 8 December 1978, sec. D, p. 1.

3. Ibid.

4. Ibid.

5. Ibid.

6. Ibid.

7. Ibid.

8. Harry Blake, interview by author, Shreveport, Louisiana, 3 August 2006.

9. Don Walker, "Council Approves Apology Resolution," *Shreveport Times,* 23 September 2003.

Chapter Seven

1. Marcia Desmond, "D'Artois Admits Destroying 3 'Boys' Files," *Shreveport Journal,* 12 May 1976, sec. A, p. 1.

2. "*Times* Newsman Discovers Police Records Missing," *Shreveport Times,* 8 May 1976, sec. A, p. 1.

3. Ibid.

4. Ibid.

5. Bill Keith, "More Gambling Arrest Records Found Missing," *Shreveport Times,* 9 May 1976, sec. A, p. 1.

6. Ibid.

7. Burns, interview.

8. Alan Stonecipher, "D'Artois Probe Is Inconclusive," *Shreveport Journal,* 5 May 1976, sec. A, p. 1.

9. Ibid.

10. Marcia Desmond, "Poll Indicates Council Approves of Allen's Request for Probe," *Shreveport Journal,* 14 May 1976, sec. C, p. 1.

11. Marcia Desmond, "Allen Pulls Kelley Off Probe; City Council Takes Over," *Shreveport Journal,* 13 May 1976, sec. A, p. 1.

12. Bill Keith, "Guste Pledges Full Probe at City Hall," *Shreveport Times,* 14 May 1976, sec. A, p. 1.

13. Ibid.

Chapter Eight

1. Marcia Desmond, "D'Artois Probe Handed to Attorney General," *Shreveport Journal,* 13 May 1976, sec. A, p. 1.

2. Ibid.

3. Alan Stonecipher, "Commissioner D'Artois Launches Counterattack," *Shreveport Journal,* 19 May 1976, sec. A, p. 1.

4. Jim Montgomery, "Shreveport's Finest," *Shreveport Times,* 13 May 1976, sec. A, p. 6.

5. Stonecipher, sec. A, p 1.

6. Ibid.

7. Ibid.

8. Jim Montgomery, "We Will Proceed," *Shreveport Times,* 23 May 1976, sec. B, p. 2.

Chapter Nine

1. J. L. Wilson, "22 Subpoenaed in D'Artois Case," *Shreveport Times,* 6 June 1976, sec. A, p. 1.
2. Ibid.
3. Ibid.
4. Bill Keith, "Guste Says D'Artois Not Required to Step Down," *Shreveport Times,* 11 June 1976, sec. A, p. 1.
5. Ibid.
6. Robert Merolla, interview by author, Bethany, Louisiana, 23 June 2006.
7. Burns, interview.
8. J. L. Wilson, "Grand Jury Indicts D'Artois," *Shreveport Times,* 11 June 1976, sec. A, p. 1.
9. Ibid.
10. Ibid.
11. Ibid.
12. Marcia Desmond, "D'Artois Won't Quit," *Shreveport Journal,* 14 June 1976, sec. A, p. 1.
13. Orland Dodson, "D'Artois Says Charges No Reason to Resign," *Shreveport Times,* 15 June 1976, sec. A, p. 1.
14. Ibid.
15. Burns, interview.
16. Kelley, interview.
17. Alan Stonecipher, "Sound Off Voting on D'Artois Ends in Virtual Tie," *Shreveport Journal,* 16 June 1976, sec. A, p. 1.
18. Ibid.
19. J. L. Wilson, "D'Artois Posts Bond After Being Booked," *Shreveport Times,* 17 June 1976, sec. A, p. 1.
20. Jim Montgomery, "Leave for D'Artois," *Shreveport Times,* 20 June 1976, sec. A, p. 4.
21. Alan Stonecipher, "Monitor, We Must," *Shreveport Journal,* 23 June 1976, sec. A, p. 4.
22. J. L. Wilson, "Grand Jury Indicts D'Artois on Three Additional Counts," *Shreveport Times,* 23 June 1976, sec. A, p. 1.
23. Marcia Desmond, "Mitigating Circumstances Cited in Lambert Case," *Shreveport Journal,* 8 October 1976, sec. A, p. 10.

Chapter Eleven

1. "D'Artois Staying in Office Despite Felony Charges," *Shreveport Journal,* 24 July 1976, sec. A, p. 11.
2. Ibid.

3. Ibid.

4. Ibid.

5. Alan Stonecipher, "D'Artois Resigns, Gives Medical Reasons," *Shreveport Journal,* 30 July 1976, sec. A, p. 1.

6. "D'Artois Resigns/The Storm Subsides," *Shreveport Journal,* 30 July 1976, sec. A, p. 6.

7. Alan Stonecipher, "DA Says Hearing Set for Monday," *Shreveport Journal,* 31 July 1976, sec. A, p. 1.

8. Alan Stonecipher, "Grand Jury Witness Says D'Artois Threatened Life," *Shreveport Journal,* 2 August 1976, sec. A, p. 1.

9. Ibid.

10. Ibid.

11. Ibid.

12. Ibid.

13. Philip Stonecipher, "D'Artois Can't Be Found After Arrest Is Ordered," *Shreveport Journal,* 3 August 1976, sec. A, p. 1.

14. Alan Stonecipher, "D'Artois Says He Will Return Today," *Shreveport Journal,* 4 August 1976, sec. A, p. 1.

15. Ibid.

16. Susan Stoler, "D'Artois Pleads Innocent to Charges, Indictments," *Shreveport Journal,* 10 August 1976, sec. A, p. 1.

Chapter Twelve

1. "D'Artois Reportedly Wanted Leslie Taken Care Of," *Shreveport Journal,* 3 September 1976, sec. A, p. 1.

2. Ibid.

3. Ibid.

4. Ibid.

5. John Hill and J. L. Wilson, "Man Quizzed in Leslie Murder," *Shreveport Times,* 3 September 1976, sec. A, p. 1.

6. Ibid.

7. Ibid.

8. Ibid.

9. Ibid.

10. Ronni Patriquin, "Guevara Says D'Artois Offered Leslie Contract," *Shreveport Journal,* 3 March 1977, sec. A, p. 1.

11. Ibid.

12. J. L. Wilson, "Brown: D'Artois Ordered Murder," *Shreveport Times,* 15 October 1976, sec. A, p. 3.

13. Ibid.

14. Ibid.

15. Alan Stonecipher, "Kelley Traces Role in D'Artois Probe," *Shreveport Journal,* 15 September 1976, sec. A, p. 16.

16. Ibid.

17. Alan Stonecipher, "D'Artois Legacy Is Factor in Safety Post Race," *Shreveport Journal,* 27 September 1976, sec. A, p. 1.

18. Ibid.

19. Ibid.

20. Ibid.

21. Jim Montgomery, "Kelley for Commissioner," *Shreveport Times,* 28 September 1976, sec. A, p. 4.

22. Marcia Desmond, "Hayes Picks Lanigan New Police Chief," *Shreveport Journal,* 15 November 1976, sec. A, p. 1.

23. Ibid.

Chapter Thirteen

1. Henry Delahunt, "Map Led Local Man to Site of Murder," *Shreveport Journal*, 18 October 1976, sec. A, p. 1.

2. Ibid.

3. Ibid.

4. Ibid.

5. Henry Delahunt, "Links to Organized Crime Found With Murder Victim," *Shreveport Journal,* 19 October 1976, sec. A, p. 1.

6. Ibid.

7. Henry Delahunt, "More Arrests Expected in Murder of Griffith," *Shreveport Journal*, 8 November 1976, sec. A, p. 1.

8. Ibid.

9. Ibid.

10. Bob Anderson, "They Took the Gamble of Killing the Big Man—Will It Pay Off?" *Shreveport Journal*, 21 September 1977.

11. Nora Norris, "2 Get Life Sentences for Conspiracy," *Baton Rouge Morning Advocate*, 7 March 1982, sec. A, p. 1.

12. Ibid.

13. Ibid.

Chapter Fourteen

1. Stanley Tiner, "The State of Shreveport's City Hall," *Shreveport Journal*, 18 March 1977, sec. A, p. 5.

2. Ibid.

3. Ibid.

4. "Arrests Due Today in Two Murders; D'Artois Named," *Shreveport Times,* 19 April 1977, sec. A, p. 1.

5. Ibid.

6. J. W. Jones, interview by author, Shreveport, Louisiana, 11 April 2006.

7. Elaine King, "Arrest Ends 8-hour Vigil," *Shreveport Times*, 20 April 1977, sec. A, p. 2.

8. Ibid.

9. Ibid.

10. Ibid.

11. John Emerich Edward Dalberg-Acton, *The Selected Writings of Lord Acton,* 3 vols., ed. J. Rufus Fears (Indianapolis: Liberty Classics, 1985-1988).

12. King, sec. A, p. 2.

13. Ibid.

14. Ibid.

15. John Hill, "D'Artois' Specially Built Cell Resembles Small Motel Room," *Shreveport Times,* 20 April 1977, sec. A, p. 7.

16. Ibid.

17. John Hill and Marsha Shuler, "D'Artois Held Without Bond," *Shreveport Times*, 21 April 1977, sec. A, p. 1.

18. Ibid.

19. "D'Artois Jailed in B.R.," *Shreveport Times*, 20 April 1977, sec. A, p. 7.

20. Jim Montgomery, "The D'Artois Case," *Shreveport Times*, 20 April 1977, sec. A, p. 10.

21. Ibid.

22. Mary Catherine Bounds, "Arrest No Reflection on City," *Shreveport Times*, 20 April 1977, sec. A, p. 1.

23. Ibid.

24. Craig Fluornoy, "It's Like Living in a Fishbowl," *Shreveport Journal*, 13 May 1977, sec. A, p. 1.

25. Ibid.

26. Ibid.

Chapter Fifteen

1. "Text of Affidavit," *Shreveport Times*, 20 April 1977, sec. A, p. 4.

2. Ibid.

3. Gibbs Adams, "Released in Leslie Case," *Baton Rouge Morning Advocate*, 11 May 1977, sec. A, p. 1

4. Bob Anderson, "U.S. Enters Jim Leslie Death Case," *Baton Rouge Morning Advocate*, 27 May 1981, sec. A, p. 1.

Chapter Sixteen
1. Ronni Patriquin, "Brown Unsure on Leslie Case Immunity," *Shreveport Journal*, 26 April 1977, sec. A, p. 1.
2. Ibid.
3. Ibid.
4. Ibid.
5. Ronni Patriquin, "3 Witnesses Won't Talk Without Immunity," *Shreveport Journal*, 10 May 1977, sec. A, p. 1.
6. Ibid.
7. Ibid.
8. Ibid.
9. John Hill, "D'Artois Released From Jail," *Shreveport Times*, 11 May 1977, sec. A, p. 1.
10. Ibid.
11. Ibid.
12. Ronni Patriquin, "D'Artois Free: Probe Continues," *Shreveport Journal*, 11 May 1977, sec. A, p. 1.
13. Associated Press, "Amiss Insists D'Artois, Gardner Guilty," *Shreveport Journal*, 12 May 1977, sec. A, p. 1.
14. John Hill, "Hearing for D'Artois Termed Almost Comical," *Shreveport Times*, 15 May 1977, sec. A, p. 1.
15. J. L. Wilson, "D'Artois Hits Amiss with $4.5 Million Suit," *Shreveport Times*, 24 May 1977, sec. A, p. 1.

Chapter Seventeen
1. "D'Artois to Undergo Surgery Wednesday," *Shreveport Journal*, 7 June 1977, sec. A, p. 1.
2. "D'Artois Condition Critical," *Shreveport Journal*, 9 June 1977, sec. A, p. 1.
3. "The Book Is Closed," *Shreveport Journal*, 13 June 1977, sec. A, p. 4.

Chapter Eighteen
1. Susan Parker, "D'Artois Declared Innocence in Letter," *Shreveport Journal*, 20 December 1978, sec. 1D.
2. Ibid.
3. Ibid.
4. Ibid.
5. Ibid.
6. Ibid.

7. Thomas Mitchell and Jim Burns, "D'Artois Family Rests Case After Hearing Amiss Testimony," *Shreveport Journal*, 18 January 1979, sec. A, p. 1.

8. Ibid.

Appendix A

1. Jay Dardenne, Louisiana secretary of state, *Governors,* public records, http://www.sos.louisiana.gov (accessed January 23, 2009).

2. Ibid.

3. Ibid.

4. A. J. Leibling, *The Earl of Louisiana* (Baton Rouge: Louisiana State University Press, 1970).

5. Tyler Bridges, *Bad Bet on the Bayou: The Rise of Gambling in Louisiana and the Fall of Governor Edwin Edwards* (New York: Farrar, Straus, and Giroux, 2001), 4.

6. Ibid.

7. Ibid.

8. "Former Louisiana Governor Edwin Edwards Convicted by Federal Jury," Cable News Network, 9 May 2000.

9. "Former Governor Edwin Edwards to be Sentenced," Cable News Network, 8 January 2000.

10. Ibid.

11. Ibid.

Appendix B

1. Ronni Patriquin and Bill Keith, "Weaver Accused Dozier of Selling Powers," *Shreveport Journal,* 18 May 1978, sec. A, p. 1.

2. Shari Dwyer, "Easy Money," *Leader's Edge,* May/June 2004.

3. "Commentary," *Gambit Weekly,* 13 March 2001.

4. Ibid.

5. Dwyer, 2004.

6. "FBI Agents Search Louisiana Representative William Jefferson's Office," Associated Press, 21 May 2006.

7. Allan Lengel and Jonathan Weisman, "For Deals, Jefferson Built Web of Firms," *Washington Post,* 5 June 2006.

8. Ibid.